AN INCLUSIVE LANGUAGE LECTIONARY

Readings for Year A

*Prepared for experimental and voluntary use in churches by
the Inclusive Language Lectionary Committee
appointed by the Division of Education and
Ministry, National Council of the Churches of
Christ in the U.S.A.*

Published for
The Cooperative Publication Association
by
John Knox Press, *Atlanta*
The Pilgrim Press, *New York*
The Westminster Press, *Philadelphia*

BOOK DESIGN BY ALICE DERR

PRINTED IN THE UNITED STATES OF AMERICA
9 8 7 6 5 4 3 2 1

Library of Congress Cataloging in Publication Data

Main entry under title:

An Inclusive language lectionary.

  Includes bibliographical references and index.
  1. Bible—Liturgical lessons, English.   2. Lectionaries—Texts.   3. Sexism in liturgical language. I. National Council of the Churches of Christ in the United States of America. Inclusive Language Lectionary Committee.
BS391.2.I52 1983   264′.34   83-16779
ISBN 0-664-24506-4 (Westminster Press : pbk.) (Year A)

Preface

All persons are equally loved, judged, and accepted by God. This belief has been promoted by the church and has its roots in the origins of the Judeo-Christian tradition. Young and old, male and female, and persons of every racial, cultural, and national background are included in the faith community. Basic to a sense of equality and inclusiveness is the recognition that God by nature transcends all categories. God is more than male or female, and is more than can be described in historically and culturally limiting terms. God's holiness and mystery are present in the biblical tradition even if the words used to describe God reflect limitations—words and language convey as best they can what is virtually impossible to describe. Seeking to express the truth about God and about God's inclusive love for all persons, the Division of Education and Ministry of the National Council of the Churches of Christ authorized the preparation of AN INCLUSIVE LANGUAGE LECTIONARY.

A Task Force on Biblical Translation was appointed by the Division of Education and Ministry to investigate how the language of the Bible presented the characteristics of God and of people. In 1980, after almost three years of study and discussion, the Task Force recommended to the Division the creation of an Inclusive Language Lectionary Committee. Twelve women and men were appointed, bringing to the Committee not only their personal commitment to the Christian faith and involvement in particular congregations but also their experience as pastors, teachers, and leaders who have relied on the Bible as their source for inspiration and for an understanding of God's word for the church today. English, worship, Old and New Testaments, theology, and education are areas of expertise provided by the Committee members. In addition, the members represent a variety of denominations and liturgical traditions. The Inclusive Language Lectionary Committee consists of Robert A. Bennett, Dianne Bergant, Victor Roland Gold (chairperson), Thomas Hoyt, Jr., Kellie C. Jones, Patrick D. Miller, Jr., Virginia Ramey Mollenkott, Sharon H. Ringe (vice-chairperson), Susan Thistlethwaite, Burton H. Throckmorton, Jr., and Barbara A. Withers. T. Herbert O'Driscoll, Marvin H. Pope, and Keith Watkins served partial terms. David Ng is the National Council of Churches' liaison to the Committee.

The Inclusive Language Lectionary Committee followed the general guidelines provided by the Division of Education and Ministry to create for use in services of worship inclusive language lectionary readings based on the Revised Standard Version of the Bible, with the text revised only in those places where male-biased or otherwise inappropriately exclusive language could be modified to reflect an inclusiveness of all persons.

The Committee worked on lectionary passages first in subcommittees. The results of this initial study (based on other translations, commentaries, Greek and Hebrew texts) were submitted to the entire Committee for thorough discussion and preliminary agreement. An Editorial Committee then reviewed all the texts for consistency of changes and agreement with guiding principles; then the Preface, Introduction, and Appendix were written. The completed manuscript was submitted to the full Committee for its final approval.

Like most other lectionaries in use today, this lectionary follows the pattern of a three-year cycle beginning with the first Sunday in Advent. This volume contains Cycle A, for first use in Advent 1983 through Pentecost 1984, based on the collation of the lectionaries presently in use, published by the Consultation on Church Union.[1] It will be followed by separate volumes for Cycle B (beginning in Advent 1984) and Cycle C (beginning in Advent 1985), based on the lectionary newly developed by the North American Committee on Calendar and Lectionary. This "common text" list of readings has the endorsement of a growing number of Protestant and Roman Catholic groups. Only in recent years have Protestant and Roman Catholic churches moved toward a common, fixed selection of readings for Sunday morning worship.

When a lectionary is used in services of worship, the people become familiar with a range of scripture, including the Old Testament, the Epistles,[2] and the Gospels. Over a three-year period, about 95 percent of the New Testament is heard, as well as a good portion of the Old Testament. Prescribed readings safeguard congregations from what might be the narrower preferences of individual ministers.

Each Sunday all congregations that read from a lectionary will hear the same scriptures. Thus the wider church, within denominations and across denominational lines, is united in its hearing and thinking and praying. A

---

[1]Pentecost 25 has been omitted because few denominations use that set of readings.
[2]"Epistles" refers in this instance to the letters of the apostles. In the lectionary, "Epistles" also designates all Lesson 2 readings, including those from Acts, Hebrews, and so forth.

lectionary provides a way for Christians consciously to live out the *church year*, which begins on the first Sunday of Advent and is followed by Christmas, Epiphany, Ash Wednesday, Lent, Passion (Palm) Sunday, Maundy Thursday, Good Friday, Easter, Ascension, and Pentecost. At least three readings are prescribed for each Sunday and for special days such as Christmas and Easter.

The Introduction which follows offers an explanation of what a lectionary is, the need for inclusive language, and how the Committee approached the bias discerned in the language of scripture. The lectionary passages, along with explanatory footnotes, form the major portion of this volume. An appendix stating a rationale for the major alternative words and phrases, and an index of the Bible passages that appear in this lectionary, complete this volume.

AN INCLUSIVE LANGUAGE LECTIONARY is offered to the church as a provisional, experimental, and responsible attempt to proclaim the biblical message in an inclusive manner. Its use is voluntary and responses are invited and can be addressed to the Division of Education and Ministry, National Council of the Churches of Christ, Room 704, 475 Riverside Drive, New York, New York 10115-0050. The hope is that no one will find that she or he has been excluded from hearing the words of promise and fulfillment. God loves and seeks to bring all people into God's community. This rendering of the lectionary texts attempts to express that message.

Introduction

Latin — lectus — to
lectio legere — read

A lectionary is a fixed selection of readings, taken from both the Old and the New Testament, to be read and heard in the churches' services of worship. A lectionary follows the church year, not the calendar year. Most lectionaries are simply indexes of readings to be used. They cite the biblical book from which the reading is taken, as well as the chapter and verses: for example, on Christmas Day, Luke 2:1-20. But this lectionary contains the selections printed in full: that is, the whole of Luke 2:1-20 is given.

It is apparent that any selection of scripture read in a service of worship has been lifted from its biblical context. In the study of the Bible, the context in which a biblical passage occurs is crucial to its interpretation. But when passages are read in a service of worship, they are read in a new context, in relation to each other and to the church year. This radical change in the context of selections differentiates a lectionary from the Bible.

A lectionary thus has a special function in the worship of the church. It does not supplant the Bible. The Bible is the church's book—created by and for the church. A lectionary is also the church's book, being a prescribed set of readings selected by the church from its scripture for its own special use in worship. The unique feature of this inclusive language lectionary is that it recasts some of the wording of the Revised Standard Version in order to provide to both reader and hearer a sense of belonging to a Christian faith community in which truly all are one in Christ.

Why inclusive language? The lectionary readings are based on the Revised Standard Version and original Greek and Hebrew texts, with the intent of reflecting the full humanity of women and men in the light of the gospel. Women have been denied full humanity by a pattern of exclusion in English usage. Consider, for example, the traditional English use of the word "man." A man is a male being, as opposed to a female being. But in common usage "man" has also meant "human being," as opposed to "animal." On the other hand, "woman" means female, but never *human being.* No word that refers to a female person identifies her with humanity. So, in the common English idiom, "man" has been defined by his humanity, but "woman" by her sex, by her relationship to man. "Woman" becomes a subgroup under "human." Man is the human race; woman is his sexual partner in traditional English usage.

This is simply one example of how language *reflects* the way in which we think but also *informs* the way in which we think: English translations of the Bible perpetuate the assumption that man is primary and woman secondary.

How the Revised Standard Version Has Been Recast

Most biblical scholars in this country agree that the RSV is the most accurate and reliable English version of the Bible. However, in this lectionary the wording of the RSV has been recast to minimize the male bias reflected in its language about human beings and language about Christ and God. For example, the word "brethren" has been rendered in this lectionary in a variety of ways, including "sisters and brothers." Formal equivalents have been adopted for other specific male-biased words and phrases. For example, "kingdom" is rendered "realm," and "king" is rendered "ruler" or "monarch." Where appropriate, additions to the text to include women have been made and noted—e.g., "Abraham [*and Sarah*]."

Male bias, however, is not unique to English translations of the Bible; it is characteristic of both the Old and the New Testament in their original languages. Both the Old Testament and the New Testament were written in languages and in cultures that were basically patriarchal; and as the English language is also patriarchal, the patriarchal character of both Testaments has slipped easily into the great English versions of the Bible.

Keeping this cultural context in mind, the Committee deliberately utilized some language that includes women even in nontraditional settings. For example, "watchman" (Ezek. 33:2) has been rendered "watcher," even though the Hebrew word clearly refers to a male sentry who protected the city or town from surprise attack. In this lectionary, women can hear themselves as those who are called to watch for the deeds of God.

In a few instances the RSV Bible committee has already avoided male bias. For example, in Rom. 7:1 the RSV has used "person" ("the law is binding on a *person*") as a translation of the Greek word *anthrōpos* (meaning "man" or "person"). But most of the time *anthrōpos* is translated "man," or, in the plural, "men." For example, Matt. 5:16 in the RSV reads, "Let your light so shine before *men*" where the meaning of "men" is obviously "people," but not male people exclusively. In this lectionary the reading of Matt. 5:16 is, "Let your light so shine before *others*"—i.e., men and women, which represents the clear intention of the words.

Male bias also appears when pronoun subjects are supplied with third person singular verbs. Compare, for example, the RSV of John 6:35-37: "Jesus said to them, 'I am the bread of life; *he* who comes to me shall not hunger, and *he* who believes in me shall never thirst . . . ; and *him* who comes to me I will not cast out." What is the intention of this passage? It surely is not that only *men* come to Jesus and believe in Jesus. Why, then, does the RSV read "he" and "him"? It is because of the assumption that "he" also means "she," though we know that it does not.

In this lectionary all readings have been recast so that no masculine word pretends to include a woman. When the scriptures are read in and to the church, they will not exclude half of those who hear. All who hear will know themselves to be equal. A major function of a lectionary is to facilitate the oral reading of the Bible in worship. To this end, pronouns have been frequently replaced by the proper names, both for clarity and to reduce the preponderance of male references. Punctuation marks have been added or changed in accordance with changes in sentence structure.

Language About Jesus Christ. Jesus was a male human being. But when the Gospel of John says, "The Word became flesh" (1:14), it does not say or imply that the Word became *male* flesh, but simply *flesh*. Of course, to "become flesh," the one from God had to become male or female, but this lectionary tries to overcome the implication that in the incarnation Jesus' *maleness* is decisive—or even relevant—for the salvation of women and men who believe. From the very beginning of the church the salvation of women has been assumed to be equal to the salvation of men.

In this lectionary the fact of Jesus' maleness is, of course, taken for granted. However, it is deemphasized, so that in hearing the gospel, the church may be reminded of the inclusiveness of all humanity in the incarnation. In reference to Jesus, the pronoun "he" is frequently replaced by the noun "Jesus." Formal equivalents for the phrases "the Son of man," "Son," and "Son of God" are "the Human One," "Child," and "Child of God." (For discussion of these terms, see the Appendix.)

Language About God. The God worshiped by the biblical authors, and worshiped in the church, is beyond sex, as God is also beyond race or any other limiting attribute. Nevertheless, biblical language used of God is frequently masculine, as the Bible's images and metaphors for God are frequently male. Yet when one says "God," it is clear that if one means *male* God, one falls into idolatry.

This lectionary tries to speak of God as beyond differentiations of sex, so that when the church hears its scripture read, it is not overwhelmed by the male metaphors, but is also allowed to hear the female metaphors for God. For example, God as mother is found in the Old Testament: "Now I will cry out like a woman in travail" (Isa. 42:14); and God is compared to a mother suckling her children (Num. 11:12); a seamstress making clothes for Israel to wear (Neh. 9:21); and a midwife attending a birth (Job 3:12; Ps. 22:9-10a; 71:6). In the New Testament, the parable of the woman seeking the lost coin (Luke 15:8-10) is a female metaphor for God.

The formal equivalent adopted in this lectionary for "God the Father" or "Father" is "God the Father [*and Mother*]" or "God the [*Mother and*] Father." The words that are an addition to the text, which may be omitted in the reading of the text, are italicized and in brackets. (For an explanation of metaphor, and of specific ways in which this lectionary has recast scriptural language about God and images for God, see the Appendix.)

Toward the Future

AN INCLUSIVE LANGUAGE LECTIONARY is a first attempt to rethink the language of scripture as inclusive of both men and women, and as such it is provisional and experimental.

Scripture is written in patriarchal language, but God is not a patriarch. According to scripture, "There is neither male nor female, for you are all one in Christ Jesus" (Gal. 3:28).

ADVENT 1

Lesson 1 ~ Isaiah 2:2-5

Isaiah speaks a prophecy concerning Judah and Jerusalem.

²It shall come to pass in the latter days
    that the mountain of the house of GOD
shall be established as the highest of the mountains,
    and shall be raised above the hills;
and all the nations shall flow to it,
³   and many peoples shall come, and say:
"Come, let us go up to the mountain of GOD,
    to the house of the God of Jacob, [*Rachel, and Leah**];
that we may be taught the ways of God
    and may walk in God's paths."
For out of Zion shall go forth the law,
    and the word of GOD from Jerusalem.
⁴God shall judge between the nations,
    and shall decide for many peoples;
and they shall beat their swords into plowshares,
    and their spears into pruning hooks;
nation shall not lift up sword against nation,
    neither shall they learn war any more.
⁵O house of Jacob, [*Rachel, and Leah**],
    come, let us walk in the light of GOD.

Lesson 2 ~ Romans 13:8-14

Paul writes to the Romans concerning the conduct of their daily lives.

⁸Owe no one anything, except to love one another; for whoever loves one's neighbor has fulfilled the law. ⁹The commandments, "You shall not commit adultery, You shall not kill, You shall not steal, You shall not covet," and any other commandment, are summed up in this sentence, "You shall love your neighbor as yourself." ¹⁰Love does no wrong to a neighbor; therefore love is the fulfilling of the law.

¹¹Besides this you know what hour it is, how it is full time now for you to wake from sleep. For salvation is nearer to us now than when we first believed; ¹²the night is far gone, the day is at hand. Let us then cast off the

---

*Addition to the text. See Appendix.

works of the night and put on the armor of the day; ¹³let us conduct ourselves becomingly as in the day, not in reveling and drunkenness, not in debauchery and licentiousness, not in quarreling and jealousy. ¹⁴But put on the Sovereign□ Jesus Christ, and make no provision for the flesh, to gratify its desires.

Gospel ~ Matthew 24:36-44

Jesus speaks to the disciples about the end times, especially the day on which the Human One will come.

³⁶But of that day and hour no one knows, not even the angels of heaven, nor the Child,◇ but God⊗ only. ³⁷As were the days of Noah, so will be the coming of the Human One.○ ³⁸ For as in those days before the flood they were eating and drinking, marrying and giving in marriage, until the day when Noah entered the ark, ³⁹and they did not know until the flood came and swept them all away, so will be the coming of the Human One.○ ⁴⁰Then two men will be in the field; one is taken and one is left. ⁴¹Two women will be grinding at the mill; one is taken and one is left. ⁴²Watch therefore, for you do not know on what day your Sovereign□ is coming. ⁴³But know this, that if the householder had known in what part of the night the thief was coming, that householder would have watched and would not have let the house be broken into. ⁴⁴Therefore you also must be ready; for the Human One○ is coming at an hour you do not expect.

□RSV *Lord.* See Appendix.
◇RSV *Son.* See Appendix.
⊗RSV *the Father.*
○RSV *Son of man.* See Appendix.

ADVENT 2

Isaiah brings a promise to Israel.

¹There shall come forth a shoot from the stump of Jesse,
and a branch shall grow out of its roots.
²And the Spirit of GOD shall rest upon this branch,
the spirit of wisdom and understanding,
the spirit of counsel and might,
the spirit of knowledge and the fear of GOD.
³And the delight of the one who comes shall be in the fear of GOD.
That one shall not judge by what the eyes see,
or decide by what the ears hear;
⁴but shall judge the poor with righteousness,
and decide with equity for the meek of the earth,
and smite the earth with words of judgment,
and slay the wicked with sentences.
⁵The coming one shall be girded with righteousness,
and girded also with faithfulness.
⁶The wolf shall dwell with the lamb,
and the leopard shall lie down with the kid,
and the calf and the lion and the fatling together,
and a little child shall lead them.
⁷The cow and the bear shall feed;
their young shall lie down together;
and the lion shall eat straw like the ox.
⁸The sucking child shall play over the hole of the asp,
and the weaned child shall put its hand on the adder's den.
⁹They shall not hurt or destroy
in all my holy mountain;
for the earth shall be full of the knowledge of GOD
as the waters cover the sea.
¹⁰In that day the root of Jesse shall stand as an ensign to the peoples that
this is the one whom the nations shall seek, whose dwellings shall be
glorious.

Paul sends a message of praise and encouragement to the Christians at Rome.

⁴Whatever was written in former days was written for our instruction, that by steadfastness and by the encouragement of the scriptures we might have hope. ⁵May the God of steadfastness and encouragement grant you to live in such harmony with one another, in accord with Christ Jesus, ⁶that together you may with one voice glorify God the Father [*and Mother**] of our Sovereign□ Jesus Christ.

⁷Welcome one another, therefore, as Christ has welcomed you, for the glory of God. ⁸For I tell you that Christ became a servant to the Jews to show God's truthfulness, in order to confirm the promises given to the ancestors in faith, ⁹and in order that the Gentiles might glorify God for showing mercy. As it is written,

"Therefore I will praise you among the Gentiles,
and sing to your name";
¹⁰and again it is said,
"Rejoice, O Gentiles, with the people of God";
¹¹and again,
"Praise the Sovereign,□ all Gentiles,
and let all the peoples praise God";
¹²and further Isaiah says,
"The root of Jesse shall come,
the one who rises to rule the Gentiles,
in whom the Gentiles shall hope."
¹³May the God of hope fill you with all joy and peace in believing, so that by the power of the Holy Spirit you may abound in hope.

Gospel ~ Matthew 3:1-12

Matthew recounts the preaching of John the Baptist.

¹In those days came John the Baptist, preaching in the wilderness of Judea, ²"Repent, for the realm* of heaven is at hand." ³For this is the one spoken of by the prophet Isaiah,

---

*Addition to the text. RSV *the God and Father*. See "Metaphor" and "God the Father and Mother" in the Appendix.
□RSV *Lord*. See Appendix.
*RSV *kingdom*. See Appendix.

"The voice of one crying in the wilderness:
Prepare the way of the Sovereign One,□
make the paths straight."

⁴Now John wore a garment of camel's hair, and a leather girdle around his waist; and his food was locusts and wild honey. ⁵Then Jerusalem and all Judea and all the region about the Jordan went out to John, ⁶and they were baptized by John in the river Jordan, confessing their sins.

⁷But seeing many of the Pharisees and Sadducees coming for baptism, John said to them, "You brood of vipers! Who warned you to flee from the wrath to come? ⁸Bear fruit that befits repentance, ⁹and do not presume to say to yourselves, 'We have Abraham as our father [*and Sarah and Hagar as our mothers**]'; for I tell you, God is able from these stones to raise up children to Abraham, [*Sarah, and Hagar**]. ¹⁰Even now the axe is laid to the root of the trees; every tree therefore that does not bear good fruit is cut down and thrown into the fire.

¹¹"I baptize you with water for repentance, but the one who is coming after me is mightier than I, whose sandals I am not worthy to carry, who will baptize you with the Holy Spirit and with fire. ¹²With winnowing fork in hand, the Sovereign will clear the threshing floor and gather the wheat into the granary, but the chaff will be burned with unquenchable fire."

□RSV *Lord*. See Appendix.
*Addition to the text. See Appendix.

ADVENT 3

Lesson 1 ~ Isaiah 35:1-10

Isaiah speaks words of promise to Israel.

¹The wilderness and the dry land shall be glad,
the desert shall rejoice and blossom;
like the crocus ²it shall blossom abundantly,
and rejoice with joy and singing.
The glory of Lebanon shall be given to it,
the majesty of Carmel and Sharon.
They shall see the glory of the SOVEREIGN ONE,
the majesty of our God.
³Strengthen the weak hands,
and make firm the feeble knees.
⁴Say to those who are of a fearful heart,
"Be strong, fear not!
Behold, your God
will come with vengeance,
with the recompense of God.
Your God will come and save you."
⁵Then the eyes of the blind shall be opened,
and the ears of the deaf unstopped;
⁶then shall the lame leap like a hart,
and the tongues of the dumb sing for joy.
For waters shall break forth in the wilderness,
and streams in the desert;
⁷the burning sand shall become a pool,
and the thirsty ground springs of water;
the haunt of jackals shall become a swamp,
the grass shall become reeds and rushes.
⁸And a highway shall be there,
and it shall be called the Holy Way;
the unclean shall not pass over it,
and fools shall not err therein.
⁹No lion shall be there,
nor shall any ravenous beast come up on it;
they shall not be found there,
but the redeemed shall walk there.
¹⁰And the ransomed of GOD shall return,
and come to Zion with singing;
everlasting joy shall be upon their heads;
they shall obtain joy and gladness,
and sorrow and sighing shall flee away.

Lesson 2 ~ James 5:7-10

James writes to advise the church about its daily life.

⁷Be patient, therefore, my friends, until the coming of the Sovereign.□ Behold, the farmer waits for the precious fruit of the earth, being patient over it until it receives the early and the late rain. ⁸You also be patient. Establish your hearts, for the coming of the Sovereign□ is at hand. ⁹Do not grumble, sisters and brothers, against one another, that you may not be judged; behold, the Judge is standing at the doors. ¹⁰As an example of suffering and patience, friends, take the prophets who spoke in the name of the Sovereign.□

Gospel ~ Matthew 11:2-11

John sends his disciples to ask Jesus if he is the Messiah.

²Now John, having heard in prison about the deeds of the Christ, sent word by his disciples ³and said to Jesus, "Are you the one who is to come, or shall we look for another?" ⁴And Jesus answered them, "Go and tell John what you hear and see: ⁵the blind receive their sight and the lame walk, lepers are cleansed and the deaf hear, and the dead are raised up, and the poor have good news preached to them. ⁶And blessed is the one who takes no offense at me."

⁷As they went away, Jesus began to speak to the crowds concerning John: "What did you go out into the wilderness to behold? A reed shaken by the wind? ⁸Why then did you go out? To see someone clothed in soft raiment? Behold, those who wear soft raiment are in royal palaces. ⁹Why then did you go out? To see a prophet? Yes, I tell you, and more than a prophet. ¹⁰This is the one of whom it is written,

'Behold, I send my messenger before your face,
who shall prepare your way before you.'

¹¹Truly, I say to you, among those born of women there has risen no one greater than John the Baptist; yet one who is least in the realm* of heaven is greater than John.

□RSV *Lord*. See Appendix.
*RSV *kingdom*. See Appendix.

ADVENT 4

Lesson 1 ～ Isaiah 7:10-17

Isaiah brings a word of assurance from God to Ahaz, ruler of Judah, in the face of a threat from the rulers of Syria.

[10]Again GOD spoke to Ahaz, [11]"Ask a sign of the SOVEREIGN ONE your God; let it be deep as Sheol or high as heaven." [12]But Ahaz said, "I will not ask, and I will not put GOD to the test." [13]And Isaiah said, "Hear then, O house of David! Is it too little for you to weary human beings, that you weary my God also? [14]Therefore God will give you a sign. Behold, a young woman shall conceive and bear a child whom she shall call Immanuel. [15]The child shall eat curds and honey when old enough to know how to refuse the evil and choose the good. [16]For before the child knows how to refuse the evil and choose the good, the land before whose two monarchs☐ you are in dread will be deserted. [17]The SOVEREIGN ONE will bring upon you and upon your people and upon your family's house such days as have not come since the day that Ephraim departed from Judah—the monarch☐ of Assyria."

Lesson 2 ～ Romans 1:1-7

The letter from Paul to the churches in Rome begins:

[1]Paul, a servant of Jesus Christ, called to be an apostle, set apart for the gospel of God [2]promised by God beforehand through the prophets in the holy scriptures, [3]the gospel concerning God's Child,◇ who was descended from David according to the flesh [4]and designated Child◇ of God in power according to the Spirit of holiness by Christ's resurrection from the dead, Jesus Christ our Sovereign,☐ [5]through whom we have received grace and apostleship to bring about the obedience of faith for the sake of the Sovereign's name among all the nations, [6]including yourselves who are called to belong to Jesus Christ;

[7]To all God's beloved in Rome, who are called to be saints:

Grace to you and peace from God our Father [*and Mother**] and from the Sovereign☐ Jesus Christ.

☐RSV v.16 *kings*; v. 17 *king*. See Appendix.
◇RSV *Son*. See Appendix.
☐RSV *Lord*. See Appendix.
*Addition to the text. See "Metaphor" and "God the Father and Mother" in the Appendix.

Gospel ~ Matthew 1:18-25

Matthew describes the birth of Jesus Christ.

[18]Now the birth of Jesus Christ took place in this way. When Jesus' mother Mary had been betrothed to Joseph, before they came together she was found to be with child of the Holy Spirit; [19]and her husband Joseph, being just and unwilling to put her to shame, resolved to divorce her quietly. [20]But as Joseph considered this, behold, an angel of God□ appeared to him in a dream, saying, "Joseph, descendant of David, do not fear to take Mary your wife, for that which is conceived in her is of the Holy Spirit; [21]she will bear a child, whose name you shall call Jesus, for this child will save the people from their sins." [22]All this took place to fulfil what the Sovereign One□ had spoken by the prophet:

[23]"Behold, a virgin shall conceive and bear a child,
   whose name shall be called Emmanuel"
(which means, God with us). [24]When Joseph woke from sleep, he did as the angel of God□ had commanded, and married Mary, [25]but knew her not until she had borne a child; and Joseph named the child Jesus.

□RSV v. 20 *the Lord;* v. 22 *Lord;* v. 24 *the Lord.* See Appendix.

CHRISTMAS DAY (FIRST PROPER)

Lesson 1 ~ Isaiah 9:1-7

Isaiah brings words of promise from God to Israel at a time when others bring only messages of doom.

¹But there will be no gloom for the land that was in anguish. In the former time God brought into contempt the land of Zebulun and the land of Naphtali, but in the latter time God will make glorious the way of the sea, the land beyond the Jordan, Galilee of the nations.
²The people who walked in gloom
    have seen a great light;
  those who dwelt in a land of deep shadows,
    on them has light shined.
³You have multiplied the nation,
    you have increased its joy;
  they rejoice before you
    as with joy at the harvest,
    as victors rejoice when they divide the spoil.
⁴For the yoke of Israel's burden,
    and the staff for its shoulder,
    the rod of its oppressor,
    you have broken as on the day of Midian.
⁵For every boot of the tramping warrior in battle tumult
    and every garment rolled in blood
    will be burned as fuel for the fire.
⁶For to us a child is born,
    to us an heir is given;
  and the government will be on the shoulder of
    that one whose name will be called
  "Wonderful Counselor, Mighty God,
    Everlasting Father [*and Mother**], Prince of Peace."
⁷Of the increase of that government and of peace
    there will be no end,
  upon the throne of David, and over David's kingdom,
    to establish it, and to uphold it
  with justice and with righteousness
    from this time forth and for evermore.
The zeal of the GOD of hosts will do this.

---

*Addition to the text. See "Metaphor" and "God the Father and Mother" in the Appendix.

Lesson 2 ~ Titus 2:11-15

The letter to Titus points to the meaning of Christ's appearance.

[11]For the grace of God has appeared for the salvation of all, [12]training us to renounce irreligion and worldly passions, and to live sober, upright, and godly lives in this world, [13]awaiting our blessed hope, the appearing of the glory of our great God and Savior Jesus Christ, [14]who gave self for us to redeem us from all iniquity and to purify for Christ's self a chosen people who are zealous for good deeds.

[15]Declare these things; exhort and reprove with all authority. Let no one disregard you.

Gospel ~ Luke 2:1-20

See Christmas Day (Second Proper)

CHRISTMAS DAY (SECOND PROPER)

Lesson 1 ~ Isaiah 62:6-12

God speaks a word of promise to Jerusalem through the prophet Isaiah.

⁶Upon your walls, O Jerusalem,
    I have set watchers;
  all the day and all the night
    they shall never be silent.
  You who put GOD in remembrance,
    take no rest,
⁷and give God no rest
    until Jerusalem is established
    and is made a praise in the earth.
⁸GOD has sworn by God's right hand
    and by God's mighty arm:
  "I will not again give your grain
    to be food for your enemies,
  and foreigners shall not drink your wine
    for which you have labored;
⁹but those who garner it shall eat it
    and praise GOD,
  and those who gather it shall drink it in the courts of my sanctuary."
¹⁰Go through, go through the gates,
    prepare the way for the people;
  build up, build up the highway,
    clear it of stones,
    lift high an ensign over the peoples.
¹¹Behold, GOD has proclaimed
    to the end of the earth:
  Say to the children of Zion,
    "Behold, your salvation comes;
  behold, God brings the reward,
    and recompense goes before the Sovereign One."
¹²And they shall be called The holy people,
    The redeemed of GOD;
  and you shall be called Sought out,
    a city not forsaken.

Lesson 2 ~ Titus 3:4-7

The author of the letter to Titus writes of how all things are changed because of the mercy of God.

⁴When the goodness and loving kindness of God our Savior appeared,
⁵we were saved, not because of deeds done by us in righteousness, but in

virtue of God's mercy, by the washing of regeneration and renewal in the Holy Spirit, ⁶which God poured out upon us richly through Jesus Christ our Savior, ⁷so that we might be justified by God's grace and become heirs in hope of eternal life.

Gospel ~ Luke 2:1-20

Luke describes the birth of Jesus Christ.

¹In those days a decree went out from Caesar Augustus that all the world should be enrolled. ²This was the first enrollment, when Quirinius was governor of Syria. ³And all went to be enrolled, each to their own city. ⁴And Joseph also went up from Galilee, from the city of Nazareth, to Judea, to the city of David, which is called Bethlehem, because he was of the house and lineage of David, ⁵to be enrolled with Mary, his betrothed, who was with child. ⁶And while they were there, the time came for her to be delivered. ⁷And she gave birth to her first-born child, whom she wrapped in swaddling cloths and laid in a manger, because there was no place for them in the inn.

⁸And in that region there were shepherds out in the field, keeping watch over their flock by night. ⁹And an angel of God□ appeared to them, and the glory of God□ shone around them, and they were filled with fear. ¹⁰And the angel said to them, "Be not afraid; for behold, I bring you good news of a great joy which will come to all the people; ¹¹for to you is born this day in the city of David a Savior, who is Christ the Sovereign.□ ¹²And this will be a sign for you: you will find a babe wrapped in swaddling cloths and lying in a manger." ¹³And suddenly there was with the angel a multitude of the heavenly host praising God and saying,

¹⁴"Glory to God in the highest,
     and on earth peace among those with whom God is pleased!"

¹⁵When the angels went away from them into heaven, the shepherds said to one another, "Let us go over to Bethlehem and see this thing that has happened, which God□ has made known to us." ¹⁶And they went with haste, and found Mary and Joseph, and the babe lying in a manger. ¹⁷And when they saw it they made known the saying which had been told them concerning this child; ¹⁸and all who heard it wondered at what the shepherds told them. ¹⁹But Mary kept all these things, pondering them in her heart. ²⁰And the shepherds returned, glorifying and praising God for all they had heard and seen, as it had been told them.

□RSV v. 9 *the Lord;* v. 11 *Lord;* v. 15 *the Lord.* See Appendix.

CHRISTMAS DAY (THIRD PROPER)

Lesson 1 ~ Isaiah 52:6-10

Isaiah brings a word of promise from God to Israel.

⁶"Therefore my people shall know my name; therefore in that day they shall know that it is I who speak; here am I."
⁷How beautiful upon the mountains
  are the feet of the one who brings good tidings,
 who publishes peace, who brings good tidings of good,
  who publishes salvation,
  who says to Zion, "Your God reigns."
⁸Hark, your watchers lift up their voice,
  together they sing for joy;
 for eye to eye they see
  the return of GOD to Zion.
⁹Break forth together into singing,
  you waste places of Jerusalem;
 for GOD has comforted God's people,
  and has redeemed Jerusalem.
¹⁰GOD has bared God's holy arm
  before the eyes of all the nations;
 and all the ends of the earth shall see
  the salvation of our God.

Lesson 2 ~ Hebrews 1:1-12

The Letter to the Hebrews begins:

¹In many and various ways God spoke of old to our forebears by the prophets; ²but in these last days God has spoken to us by a Child,° whom God appointed the heir of all things, through whom also God created the world. ³This Child, by whose word of power the universe is upheld, reflects the glory of God and bears the very stamp of God's nature. Having made purification for sins, the Child sat down at the right hand of the Majesty on high, ⁴having become as much superior to angels as the name the Child has obtained is more excellent than theirs.
⁵For to what angel did God ever say,
 "You are my Child,°
 today I have begotten you"?

°RSV *Son.* See Appendix.

Or again,
"I will be to the Child a parent,
and the Child shall be my very own"?
[6]And again, when bringing the first-born into the world, God says,
"Let all God's angels worship the Child."
[7]Of the angels it is said,
"Who makes God's angels winds,
and God's servants flames of fire."
[8]But of the Child° it is said,
"Your throne, O God, is for ever and ever,
the righteous scepter is the scepter of your realm.*
[9]You have loved righteousness and hated lawlessness;
therefore God, your God, has anointed you
with the oil of gladness beyond your comrades."
[10]And,
"You, O Sovereign One,□ founded the earth in the beginning,
and the heavens are the work of your hands;
[11]they will perish, but you remain;
they will all grow old like a garment,
[12]like a mantle you will roll them up,
and they will be changed.
But you are the same,
and your years will never end."

Gospel ~ John 1:1-18

John unfolds the mystery of the incarnation.

[1]In the beginning was the Word, and the Word was with God, and the Word was God. [2]The Word was in the beginning with God; [3]all things were made through the Word, and without the Word was not anything made that was made. [4]In the Word was life, and the life was the light of all. [5]The light shines in the darkness, and the darkness has not overcome it.

[6]There was a man sent from God, whose name was John. [7]John came for testimony, to bear witness to the light, that all might believe through him. [8]John was not the light, but came to bear witness to the light.

[9]The true light that enlightens every one was coming into the world. [10]The Word was in the world, and the world was made through the Word,

---

°RSV *Son.* See Appendix.
*RSV *kingdom.* See Appendix.
□RSV *Lord.* See Appendix.

yet the world did not know the Word. ¹¹The Word came to the Word's own, but those to whom the Word came did not receive the Word. ¹²But to all who did receive the Word, who believed in the name of the Word, power was given to become children of God; ¹³who were born, not of blood nor of the will of the flesh nor of human will, but of God.

¹⁴And the Word became flesh and dwelt among us, full of grace and truth; we have beheld the Word's glory, glory as of the only Child° from [God] the Father [and Mother*]. ¹⁵(John bore witness to the Child, and cried, "This was the one of whom I said, 'The one who comes after me ranks before me, for that one was before me.' ") ¹⁶And from the fulness of the Child have we all received, grace upon grace. ¹⁷For the law was given through Moses; grace and truth came through Jesus Christ. ¹⁸No one has ever seen God; the only Child,° who is in the bosom of [God] the [Mother and*] Father, that one has made God known.

°RSV *Son*. See Appendix.
*Addition to the text. See "Metaphor" and "God the Father and Mother" in the Appendix.

CHRISTMAS 1

Lesson 1 ~ Isaiah 63:7-9

Isaiah writes of God's compassion.

⁷I will recount the steadfast love of GOD,
    the praises of the SOVEREIGN ONE,
according to all that GOD has granted us,
    and the great goodness to the house of Israel
which God has granted them according to God's mercy,
    according to the abundance of God's steadfast love.
⁸For God said, Surely they are my people,
    children who will not deal falsely;
    and God became their Savior.
⁹In all their affliction God was afflicted,
    and the angel of God's presence saved them;
in love and in pity God redeemed them,
    lifted them up and carried them all the days of old.

Lesson 1 (alternate) ~ Ecclesiastes 3:1-9, 14-17

The preacher speaks of times and seasons.

¹For everything there is a season, and a time for every matter under
heaven:
    ²a time to be born, and a time to die;
    a time to plant, and a time to pluck up what is planted;
    ³a time to kill, and a time to heal;
    a time to break down, and a time to build up;
    ⁴a time to weep, and a time to laugh;
    a time to mourn, and a time to dance;
    ⁵a time to cast away stones, and a time to gather stones together;
    a time to embrace, and a time to refrain from embracing;
    ⁶a time to seek, and a time to lose;
    a time to keep, and a time to cast away;
    ⁷a time to rend, and a time to sew;
    a time to keep silence, and a time to speak;
    ⁸a time to love, and a time to hate;
    a time for war, and a time for peace.
    ⁹What gain have the workers from their toil? . . .
    ¹⁴I know that whatever God does endures for ever; nothing can be
added to it, nor anything taken from it; God has made it so, in order that

people should fear before God. ¹⁵That which is, already has been; that which is to be, already has been; and God seeks what has been driven away.

¹⁶Moreover I saw under the sun that in the place of justice, even there was wickedness, and in the place of righteousness, even there was wickedness. ¹⁷I said in my heart, God will judge the righteous and the wicked, for God has appointed a time for every matter, and for every work.

Lesson 2 ~ Galatians 4:4-7

Paul writes to the Galatians about the time of Christ's coming.

⁴But when the time had fully come, God sent forth the Child,° born of woman, born under the law, ⁵to redeem those who were under the law, so that we might receive adoption as children. ⁶And because you are children, God has sent the Spirit of the Child° into our hearts, crying, "[*God! my Mother and***] Father!" ⁷So through God you are no longer a slave but a child, and if a child then an heir.

Gospel ~ John 1:1-18

See Christmas Day (Third Proper)

°RSV *Son.* See Appendix.
**RSV "*Abba! Father!*" The word "*Abba!*" is an intimate form, and Jesus' use of this term to refer to God was radically nontraditional. This warrants the use of nontraditional intimate language in contemporary reference to God. See also Rom. 8:15 (Lent 5, Lesson 2).

CHRISTMAS 2

Lesson 1 ~ Isaiah 61:10–62:3

Isaiah extols the glory of God.

¹⁰I will greatly rejoice in the SOVEREIGN ONE,
    my soul shall exult in my God,
who has clothed me with the garments of salvation,
    and covered me with the robe of righteousness,
as a bridegroom decks himself with a garland,
    and as a bride adorns herself with her jewels.
¹¹For as the earth brings forth its shoots,
    and as a garden causes what is sown in it to spring up,
so the Sovereign GOD will cause righteousness and praise
    to spring forth before all the nations.
^{62:1}For Zion's sake I will not keep silent,
    and for Jerusalem's sake I will not rest,
until its vindication goes forth as brightness,
    and its salvation as a burning torch.
²The nations shall see your vindication,
    and all the monarchs[□] your glory;
and you shall be called by a new name
    which the mouth of GOD will give.
³You shall be a crown of beauty in the hand of the SOVEREIGN ONE,
    and a royal diadem in the hand of your God.

Lesson 1 (alternate) ~ Ecclesiasticus (Sirach) 24:1-2, 8-12

Sirach writes of wisdom, God's agent in creation.

¹Wisdom will praise herself,
    and will glory in the midst of her people.
²In the assembly of the Most High she will open her mouth,
    and in the presence of the host of the Most High she will glory: . . .
⁸"Then the Creator of all things gave me a commandment,
    and the one who created me assigned a place for my tent,
and said, 'Make your dwelling in Jacob,
    and in Israel receive your inheritance.'

□RSV *kings.* See Appendix.

^{9}From eternity, in the beginning, the Most High created me,
  and for eternity I was created.
^{10}In the holy tabernacle I ministered before the Most High,
  and so I was established in Zion.
^{11}In the beloved city likewise I was given a resting place,
  and in Jerusalem was my dominion.
^{12}So I took root in an honored people,
  in the portion of the Most High, who is their inheritance."

Lesson 2 ~ Ephesians 1:3-6, 15-23

The Letter to the Ephesians begins by praising God's glorious grace in Jesus Christ.

^{3}Blessed be God the Father [*and Mother**] of our Sovereign$^\square$ Jesus Christ, who has blessed us in Christ with every spiritual blessing in the heavenly places, ^{4}even as God chose us in Christ before the foundation of the world, that we should be holy and blameless before God, ^{5}who destined us in love to be God's children through Jesus Christ, according to the purpose of God's will, ^{6}to the praise of God's glorious grace freely bestowed on us in the Beloved. . . .

^{15}For this reason, because I have heard of your faith in the Sovereign$^\square$ Jesus and your love toward all the saints, ^{16}I do not cease to give thanks for you, remembering you in my prayers, ^{17}that the God of our Sovereign$^\square$ Jesus Christ, the Father [*and Mother**] of glory, may give you a spirit of wisdom and of revelation in the knowledge of God, ^{18}having the eyes of your hearts enlightened, that you may know what is the hope to which you have been called, what are the riches of God's glorious inheritance in the saints, ^{19}and what is the immeasurable greatness of God's power in us who believe, according to the working of God's great might ^{20}which was accomplished in Christ when God raised Christ from the dead and made Christ sit at the right hand in the heavenly places, ^{21}far above all rule and authority and power and dominion, and above every name that is named, not only in this age but also in that which is to come; ^{22}and God has put all things under Christ's feet and has made Christ the head over all things for the church, ^{23}which is the body of Christ, the fulness of the one who fills all in all.

---

*Addition to the text. RSV v. 3 *the God and Father;* v. 17 *the Father.* See "Metaphor" and "God the Father and Mother" in the Appendix.
$^\square$RSV *Lord.* See Appendix.

After the visit of the magi, Joseph and Mary depart into Egypt with their child.

[13]Now when the magi had departed, behold, an angel of God□ appeared to Joseph in a dream and said, "Rise, take the child and his mother, and flee to Egypt, and remain there till I tell you; for Herod is about to search for the child, to destroy him." [14]And Joseph rose and took the child and his mother by night, and departed to Egypt, [15]and remained there until the death of Herod. This was to fulfil what God□ had spoken by the prophet, "Out of Egypt have I called my child.◇" . . .

[19]But when Herod died, behold, an angel of God□ appeared in a dream to Joseph in Egypt, saying, [20]"Rise, take the child and his mother, and go to the land of Israel, for those who sought the child's life are dead." [21]And Joseph rose and took the child and his mother, and went to the land of Israel. [22]But hearing that Archelaus reigned over Judea in place of his father Herod, Joseph was afraid to go there, and being warned in a dream, withdrew to the district of Galilee. [23]And Joseph went and dwelt in a city called Nazareth, that what was spoken by the prophets might be fulfilled, "There shall come forth a Nazarene."

□RSV *the Lord*. See Appendix.
◇RSV *son*. See Appendix.

EPIPHANY

Lesson 1 ~ Isaiah 60:1-6

Isaiah tells of the coming of God's glory to the people.

¹Arise, shine; for your light has come,
and the glory of GOD has risen upon you.
²For behold, shadows shall cover the earth,
and thick shadows the peoples;
but GOD will arise upon you,
and the glory of God will be seen upon you.
³And nations shall come to your light,
and rulers⊡ to the brightness of your rising.
⁴Lift up your eyes round about, and see;
they all gather together, they come to you;
your sons shall come from far,
and your daughters shall be carried in the arms.
⁵Then you shall see and be radiant,
your heart shall thrill and rejoice;
because the abundance of the sea shall be turned to you,
the wealth of the nations shall come to you.
⁶A multitude of camels shall cover you,
the young camels of Midian and Ephah;
all those from Sheba shall come.
They shall bring gold and frankincense,
and shall proclaim the praise of GOD.

Lesson 2 ~ Ephesians 3:1-12

The Ephesians learn about the ministry which is rooted in Christ.

¹For this reason I, Paul, a prisoner for Christ Jesus on behalf of you Gentiles—²assuming that you have heard of the stewardship of God's grace that was given to me for you, ³how the mystery was made known to me by revelation, as I have written briefly. ⁴When you read this you can perceive my insight into the mystery of Christ, ⁵which was not made known to the human race in other generations as it has now been revealed to Christ's holy apostles and prophets by the Spirit; ⁶that is, how the Gentiles are joint

---

⊡RSV *kings.* See Appendix.

heirs, members of the same body, and partakers of the promise in Christ Jesus through the gospel.

⁷Of this gospel I was made a minister according to the gift of God's grace which was given me by the working of God's power. ⁸To me, though I am the very least of all the saints, this grace was given, to preach to the Gentiles the unsearchable riches of Christ, ⁹and to make every one see what is the plan of the mystery hidden for ages in God who created all things;¹⁰that through the church the manifold wisdom of God might now be made known to the principalities and powers in the heavenly places. ¹¹This was according to the eternal purpose which God has realized in Christ Jesus our Sovereign,□ ¹²in whom we have boldness and confidence of access through our faith in Christ.

Gospel ~ Matthew 2:1-12

Matthew describes the visit of the magi.

¹Now when Jesus was born in Bethlehem of Judea in the days of Herod the king, behold, magi from the East came to Jerusalem, saying, ²"Where is the one who has been born ruler⧠ of the Jews? For we have seen the star in the East, and have come to worship the new-born child." ³And hearing this, Herod the king was troubled, and all Jerusalem as well; ⁴and assembling all the chief priests and scribes of the people, he inquired of them where the Christ was to be born. ⁵They told Herod, "In Bethlehem of Judea; for so it is written by the prophet:
⁶'And you, O Bethlehem, in the land of Judah,
  are by no means least among the rulers of Judah;
  for from you shall come a ruler
  who will govern my people Israel.' "
⁷Then Herod summoned the magi secretly, ascertained from them what time the star appeared, ⁸and sent them to Bethlehem, saying, "Go and search diligently, and when you have found the babe bring me word, that I too may come and worship him." ⁹When they had heard the king they went their way; and lo, the star which they had seen in the East went before them, till it came to rest over the place where the child was. ¹⁰When they saw the star, they rejoiced exceedingly with great joy; ¹¹and going into the house they saw the child with Mary his mother, and they fell down and worshiped him. Then, opening their treasures, they offered the child gifts, gold and frankincense and myrrh. ¹²And being warned in a dream not to return to Herod, they departed to their own country by another way.

□RSV *Lord*. See Appendix.
⧠RSV *king*. See Appendix.

BAPTISM OF OUR SOVEREIGN

Lesson 1 ~ Isaiah 42:1-9

God speaks through the prophet Isaiah about God's servant.

¹Behold my servant, whom I uphold,
   my chosen, in whom my soul delights;
 I have put my Spirit upon my servant,
   who will bring forth justice to the nations.
²My servant will not cry or speak out,
   nor be heard in the street;
³a bruised reed my servant will not break,
   nor quench a dimly burning wick,
   but will faithfully bring forth justice.
⁴My servant will not fail or be discouraged
   till justice has been established in the earth;
   and the coastlands wait for the servant's law.
⁵Thus says God, the SOVEREIGN ONE,
   who created the heavens and stretched them out,
   who spread forth the earth and what comes from it,
 who gives breath to the people upon it
   and spirit to those who walk in it:
⁶"I am the SOVEREIGN ONE, I have called you in righteousness,
   I have taken you by the hand and kept you;
 I have given you as a covenant to the people,
   a light to the nations,
⁷to open the eyes that are blind,
 to bring out the prisoners from the dungeon,
   from the prison those who sit in gloom.
⁸I am the SOVEREIGN ONE, that is my name;
   my glory I give to no other,
   nor my praise to graven images.
⁹Behold, the former things have come to pass,
   and new things I now declare;
 before they spring forth
   I tell you of them."

Lesson 2 ~ Acts 10:34-38

A centurion named Cornelius, a Gentile, comes to Peter to learn about the faith.

³⁴Peter proclaimed: "Truly I perceive that God shows no partiality, ³⁵but in every nation any one who fears God and does what is right is acceptable to God. ³⁶You know the word which God sent to Israel, preaching good news of peace by Jesus Christ (Christ is Sovereign□ of all), ³⁷the word which was proclaimed throughout all Judea, beginning from Galilee after the baptism which John preached: ³⁸how God anointed Jesus of Nazareth with the Holy Spirit and with power; how Jesus went about doing good and healing all that were oppressed by the devil, for God was with Jesus.

Gospel ~ Matthew 3:13-17

Matthew recounts what happened immediately after Jesus was baptized by John.

¹³Then Jesus came from Galilee to the Jordan to be baptized by John. ¹⁴John would have prevented Jesus, saying, "I need to be baptized by you, and do you come to me?" ¹⁵But Jesus answered, "Let it be so now; for thus it is fitting for us to fulfil all righteousness." Then John consented. ¹⁶And having been baptized, Jesus went up immediately from the water, and behold, the heavens were opened and Jesus saw the Spirit of God descending like a dove, and alighting on him; ¹⁷and lo, a voice from heaven, saying, "This is my beloved Child,◇ with whom I am well pleased."

□RSV *Lord.* See Appendix.
◇RSV *Son.* See Appendix.

EPIPHANY 2

Lesson 1 ~ Isaiah 49:1-7

The servant of God speaks through the prophet Isaiah.

¹Listen to me, O coastlands,
  and hearken, you peoples from afar.
God called me from the womb,
  from the body of my mother God named my name.
²God made my mouth like a sharp sword,
  in the shadow of God's hand I was hidden;
God made me a polished arrow,
  in the quiver I was hidden away.
³And God said to me, "You are my servant,
  Israel, in whom I will be glorified."
⁴But I said, "I have labored in vain,
  I have spent my strength for nothing and vanity;
yet surely my right is with the SOVEREIGN ONE,
  and my recompense with my God."
⁵And now GOD says,
  who formed me from the womb to be God's servant,
to bring Jacob back to the Sovereign One,
  and that Israel might be gathered to God,
for I am honored in the eyes of the SOVEREIGN ONE,
  and my God has become my strength—
⁶God says:
"It is too light a thing that you should be my servant
  to raise up the tribes of Jacob
  and to restore the preserved of Israel;
I will give you as a light to the nations,
  that my salvation may reach to the end of the earth."
⁷Thus says the SOVEREIGN ONE,
  the Redeemer of Israel and Israel's Holy One,
to one deeply despised, abhorred by the nations,
  the servant of rulers:
"Monarchs□ shall see and arise;
  rulers,** and they shall prostrate themselves;
because of the SOVEREIGN ONE, who is faithful,
  the Holy One of Israel, who has chosen you."

□RSV *Kings*. See Appendix.
**RSV *princes*.

Lesson 2 ~ 1 Corinthians 1:1-9

The First Letter of Paul to the Corinthians begins:

¹Paul, called by the will of God to be an apostle of Christ Jesus, and our brother Sosthenes,

²To the church of God which is at Corinth, to those sanctified in Christ Jesus, called to be saints together with all those who in every place call on the name of our Sovereign□ Jesus Christ, both their Sovereign□ and ours:

³Grace to you and peace from God our Father [*and Mother**] and from the Sovereign□ Jesus Christ.

⁴I give thanks to God always for you because of the grace of God which was given you in Christ Jesus, ⁵that in every way you were enriched in Christ with all speech and all knowledge—⁶even as the testimony to Christ was confirmed among you—⁷so that you are not lacking in any spiritual gift, as you wait for the revealing of our Sovereign□ Jesus Christ; ⁸who will sustain you to the end, guiltless in the day of our Sovereign□ Jesus Christ. ⁹God is faithful, by whom you were called into the community of God's Child,◇ Jesus Christ our Sovereign.□

Gospel ~ John 1:29-41

John's baptism has attracted the attention of the Pharisees. They investigate the meaning of baptism, and Jesus' identity.

²⁹John saw Jesus approaching, and said, "Behold, the Lamb of God, who takes away the sin of the world! ³⁰This is the one of whom I said, 'After me comes a person who ranks before me, for that one was before me.' ³¹I myself did not know who it was; but for this I came baptizing with water, that the one who was to come might be revealed to Israel." ³²And John bore witness, "I saw the Spirit descend as a dove from heaven, and it remained on him. ³³I myself did not know who it was; but the one who sent me to baptize with water said to me, 'The person on whom you see the Spirit descend and remain, this is the one who baptizes with the Holy Spirit.' ³⁴And I have seen and have borne witness that this is the Child ◇ of God."

³⁵The next day again John was standing with two of his disciples; ³⁶and he looked at Jesus walking by, and said, "Behold, the Lamb of God!" ³⁷The two disciples heard John say this, and they followed Jesus. ³⁸Jesus turned, and saw them following, and said to them, "What do you seek?" And they

---

□RSV *Lord.* See Appendix.
*Addition to the text. See "Metaphor" and "God the Father and Mother" in the Appendix.
◇RSV *Son.* See Appendix.

answered, "Rabbi" (which means Teacher), "where are you staying?" [39]Jesus said to them, "Come and see." The two disciples came and saw where Jesus was staying; and they stayed there that day, for it was about the tenth hour. [40]One of the two who heard John speak, and followed Jesus, was Andrew, Simon Peter's brother. [41]Andrew first found his brother Simon, and said to him, "We have found the Messiah" (which means Christ).

EPIPHANY 3

Lesson 1 ~ Isaiah 9:1-4

Isaiah brings a word of promise from God to Israel.

¹But there will be no gloom for the land that was in anguish. In the former time God brought into contempt the land of Zebulun and the land of Naphtali, but in the latter time God will make glorious the way of the sea, the land beyond the Jordan, Galilee of the nations.
²The people who walked in gloom
    have seen a great light;
those who dwelt in a land of deep shadows,
    on them has light shined.
³You have multiplied the nation,
    you have increased its joy;
they rejoice before you
    as with joy at the harvest,
    as victors rejoice when they divide the spoil.
⁴For the yoke of Israel's burden,
    and the staff for its shoulder,
    the rod of its oppressor,
    you have broken as on the day of Midian.

Lesson 1 (alternate) ~ Amos 3:1-8

The Word of God is spoken against Israel through the prophet Amos.

¹Hear this word that GOD has spoken against you, O people of Israel, against the whole family which I brought up out of the land of Egypt:
²"You only have I known
    of all the families of the earth;
therefore I will punish you
    for all your iniquities.
³Do two walk together,
    unless they have made an appointment?
⁴Does a lion roar in the forest,
    when it has no prey?
Does a young lion cry out from its den,
    if it has taken nothing?
⁵Does a bird fall in a snare on the earth,
    when there is no trap for it?

Does a snare spring up from the ground,
  when it has taken nothing?
⁶Is a trumpet blown in a city,
  and the people are not afraid?
Does evil befall a city,
  unless GOD has done it?
⁷Surely the Sovereign GOD does nothing,
  without revealing the secret
  to God's servants the prophets.
⁸The lion has roared;
  who will not fear?
The Sovereign GOD has spoken;
  who can but prophesy?"

Lesson 2 ~ 1 Corinthians 1:10-17

Paul pleads with the Corinthians to agree with each other and not to follow party leaders in the church.

¹⁰I appeal to you, sisters and brothers, by the name of our Sovereign□ Jesus Christ, that all of you agree and that there be no dissensions among you, but that you be united in the same mind and the same judgment. ¹¹For it has been reported to me by Chloe's people that there is quarreling among you, my friends. ¹²What I mean is that each of you says, "I belong to Paul," or "I belong to Apollos," or "I belong to Cephas," or "I belong to Christ." ¹³Is Christ divided? Was Paul crucified for you? Or were you baptized in the name of Paul? ¹⁴I am thankful that I baptized none of you except Crispus and Gaius; ¹⁵lest any one should say that you were baptized in my name. ¹⁶(I did baptize also the household of Stephanas. Beyond that, I do not know whether I baptized any one else.) ¹⁷For Christ did not send me to baptize but to preach the gospel, and not with eloquent wisdom, lest the cross of Christ be emptied of its power.

□RSV *Lord.* See Appendix.

Jesus has returned from the time of temptation in the wilderness, and is about to begin his public ministry.

¹²Now having heard that John had been arrested, Jesus withdrew into Galilee; ¹³and leaving Nazareth, Jesus went and dwelt in Capernaum by the sea, in the territory of Zebulun and Naphtali, ¹⁴that what was spoken by the prophet Isaiah might be fulfilled:
¹⁵"The land of Zebulun and the land of Naphtali,
　　toward the sea, across the Jordan,
　　Galilee of the Gentiles—
¹⁶the people who sat in deep gloom
　　have seen a great light,
　　and for those who sat in the region and shadow of death
　　light has dawned."
¹⁷From that time Jesus began to preach, saying, "Repent, for the realm* of heaven is at hand."
¹⁸Then walking by the Sea of Galilee, Jesus saw two brothers, Simon who is called Peter and Andrew his brother, casting a net into the sea; for they were fishers. ¹⁹And Jesus said to them, "Follow me, and I will make you fishers of women and men." ²⁰Immediately they left their nets and followed him. ²¹And going on from there Jesus saw two other brothers, James the son of Zebedee and John his brother, in the boat with Zebedee their father, mending their nets, and Jesus called them. ²²Immediately they left the boat and their father, and followed Jesus.
²³And Jesus went about all Galilee, teaching in their synagogues and preaching the gospel of the realm of God,** and healing every disease and every infirmity among the people.

---

*RSV *kingdom.* See Appendix.
**The phrase *gospel of the kingdom* is peculiar to Matthew (4:23; 9:35; 24:14). In each of these cases it is rendered in this lectionary as "gospel of the realm of God."

EPIPHANY 4

The God of Israel has a controversy with the people.

¹Hear what GOD says:
Arise, plead your case before the mountains,
   and let the hills hear your voice.
²Hear, you mountains, the controversy of GOD,
   and you enduring foundations of the earth;
for GOD has a controversy with the people,
   and will contend with Israel.
³"O my people, what have I done to you?
   In what have I wearied you? Answer me!
⁴For I brought you up from the land of Egypt,
   and redeemed you from the house of bondage;
and I sent before you Moses,
   Aaron, and Miriam.
⁵O my people, remember what Balak king of Moab devised,
   and what Balaam the son of Beor answered Balak,
and what happened from Shittim to Gilgal,
   that you may know the saving acts of GOD."
⁶"With what shall I come before the SOVEREIGN ONE,
   and bow myself before God on high?
Shall I come before God with burnt offerings,
   with calves a year old?
⁷Will GOD be pleased with thousands of rams,
   with ten thousands of rivers of oil?
Shall I give my first-born for my transgression,
   the fruit of my body for the sin of my soul?"
⁸God has showed you, O people, what is good;
   and what does the SOVEREIGN ONE require of you
but to do justice, and to love kindness,
   and to walk humbly with your God?

Lesson 1 (alternate) ~ Zephaniah 2:3; 3:11-13

The judgment of the Sovereign of Israel is proclaimed by the prophet Zephaniah.

³Seek the SOVEREIGN ONE, all you humble of the land,
    who do God's commands;
  seek righteousness, seek humility;
    perhaps you may be hidden
    on the day of the wrath of GOD. . . .
3:11"On that day you shall not be put to shame
    because of the deeds by which you have rebelled against me;
  for then I will remove from your midst
    your proudly exultant ones,
  and you shall no longer be haughty
    in my holy mountain.
¹²For I will leave in the midst of you
    a people humble and lowly.
  They shall seek refuge in the name of the SOVEREIGN ONE,
13   those who are left in Israel;
  they shall do no wrong
    and utter no lies,
  nor shall there be found in their mouth
    a deceitful tongue.
  For they shall pasture and lie down,
    and none shall make them afraid."

Lesson 2 ~ 1 Corinthians 1:18-31

Paul writes to the Corinthian church about the wisdom of God.

¹⁸For the word of the cross is folly to those who are perishing, but to us who are being saved it is the power of God. ¹⁹For it is written,
    "I will destroy the wisdom of the wise,
    and the cleverness of the clever I will thwart."
²⁰Where is the wise one? Where is the scribe? Where is the debater of this age? Has not God made foolish the wisdom of the world? ²¹For since, in the wisdom of God, the world did not know God through wisdom, it pleased God through the folly of what we preach to save those who believe. ²²For Jews demand signs and Greeks seek wisdom, ²³but we preach Christ crucified, a stumbling block to Jews and folly to Gentiles, ²⁴but to those who are called, both Jews and Greeks, Christ the power of God and the wisdom of God. ²⁵For the foolishness of God is wiser than human wisdom, and the weakness of God is stronger than human strength.

²⁶For consider your call, my friends; not many of you were wise according to worldly standards, not many were powerful, not many were of noble birth; ²⁷but God chose what is foolish in the world to shame the wise, God chose what is weak in the world to shame the strong, ²⁸God chose what is low and despised in the world, even things that are not, to bring to nothing things that are, ²⁹so that no human being might boast in the presence of God. ³⁰God is the source of your life in Christ Jesus, whom God made our wisdom, our righteousness and sanctification and redemption; ³¹therefore, as it is written, "Let the one who boasts, boast of the Sovereign."□

Gospel ~ Matthew 5:1-12

In the Sermon on the Mount, Jesus teaches about blessedness.

¹Seeing the crowds, Jesus went up on the mountain and sat down; and the disciples came to him. ²And Jesus opened his mouth and taught them, saying:
³"Blessed are the poor in spirit, for theirs is the realm* of heaven.
⁴"Blessed are those who mourn, for they shall be comforted.
⁵"Blessed are the meek, for they shall inherit the earth.
⁶"Blessed are those who hunger and thirst for righteousness, for they shall be satisfied.
⁷"Blessed are the merciful, for they shall obtain mercy.
⁸"Blessed are the pure in heart, for they shall see God.
⁹"Blessed are the peacemakers, for they shall be called children of God.
¹⁰"Blessed are those who are persecuted for righteousness' sake, for theirs is the realm* of heaven.
¹¹"Blessed are you when others revile you and persecute you and utter all kinds of evil against you falsely on my account. ¹²Rejoice and be glad, for your reward is great in heaven, for so the prophets who were before you were persecuted."

□RSV *Lord.* See Appendix.
*RSV *kingdom.* See Appendix.

EPIPHANY 5

Lesson 1 ~ Isaiah 58:5-10

What is required of those who worship God is not fasting but justice.

⁵Is such the fast that I choose,
    a day for you to humble yourself?
Is it to bow down your head like a rush,
    and to spread sackcloth and ashes under you?
Will you call this a fast,
    and a day acceptable to GOD?
⁶Is not this the fast that I choose:
    to loose the bonds of wickedness,
    to undo the thongs of the yoke,
to let the oppressed go free,
    and to break every yoke?
⁷Is it not to share your bread with the hungry,
    and bring the homeless poor into your house;
when you see the naked, to cover them,
    and not to hide yourself from your own flesh?
⁸Then shall your light break forth like the dawn,
    and your healing shall spring up speedily;
your righteousness shall go before you,
    the glory of GOD shall be your rear guard.
⁹Then you shall call, and GOD will answer;
    you shall cry, and the Sovereign One will say, Here I am.
If you take away from the midst of you the yoke,
    the pointing of the finger, and speaking wickedness,
¹⁰if you pour yourself out for the hungry
    and satisfy the desire of the afflicted,
then shall your light rise in the midnight
    and your gloom be as the noonday.

Lesson 2 ~ 1 Corinthians 2:1-5

Paul testifies to the power of God.

¹When I came to you, brothers and sisters, I did not come proclaiming to you the testimony of God in lofty words or wisdom. ²For I decided to know nothing among you except Jesus Christ and that one crucified. ³And I was with you in weakness and in much fear and trembling; ⁴and my speech and my message were not in plausible words of wisdom, but in

demonstration of the Spirit and of power, ⁵that your faith might not rest in human wisdom but in the power of God.

Gospel ∼ Matthew 5:13-20

Jesus teaches about the righteousness of the realm of God.

¹³You are the salt of the earth; but if salt has lost its taste, how shall its saltness be restored? It is no longer good for anything except to be thrown out and trodden under foot.

¹⁴You are the light of the world. A city set on a hill cannot be hid. ¹⁵No one lights a lamp and puts it under a bushel, but on a stand, and it gives light to all in the house. ¹⁶Let your light so shine before others, that they may see your good works and give glory to [God] your Father [and Mother*] who is in heaven.

¹⁷Think not that I have come to abolish the law and the prophets; I have come not to abolish them but to fulfil them. ¹⁸For truly, I say to you, till heaven and earth pass away, not an iota, not a dot, will pass from the law until all is accomplished. ¹⁹Whoever then relaxes one of the least of these commandments and teaches others to do so, shall be called least in the realm* of heaven; but whoever does them and teaches them shall be called great in the realm* of heaven. ²⁰For I tell you, unless your righteousness exceeds that of the scribes and Pharisees, you will never enter the realm* of heaven.

------

*Addition to the text. See "Metaphor" and "God the Father and Mother" in the Appendix.
*RSV *kingdom.* See Appendix.

EPIPHANY 6

Lesson 1 ~ Deuteronomy 30:15-20

Israel must choose between good and evil, life and death.

¹⁵See, I have set before you this day life and good, death and evil. ¹⁶If you obey the commandments of the SOVEREIGN ONE your God which I command you this day, by loving the SOVEREIGN ONE your God, by walking in God's ways, and by keeping God's commandments and statutes and ordinances, then you shall live and multiply, and the SOVEREIGN ONE your God will bless you in the land which you are entering to take possession of it. ¹⁷But if your heart turns away, and you will not hear, but are drawn away to worship other gods and serve them, ¹⁸I declare to you this day, that you shall perish; you shall not live long in the land which you are going over the Jordan to enter and possess. ¹⁹I call heaven and earth to witness against you this day, that I have set before you life and death, blessing and curse; therefore choose life, that you and your descendants may live, ²⁰loving the SOVEREIGN ONE your God, obeying God's voice, and cleaving to God; for that means life to you and length of days, that you may dwell in the land which GOD swore to your ancestors, to Abraham [*and Sarah**], to Isaac [*and Rebecca**], and to Jacob, [*and Leah, and Rachel**], to give them.

Lesson 1 (alternate) ~ Ecclesiasticus (Sirach) 15:15-20

God gives human beings freedom of will.

¹⁵If you will, you can keep the commandments,
  and to act faithfully is a matter of your own choice.
¹⁶God has placed before you fire and water:
  stretch out your hand for whichever you wish.
¹⁷Before each one are life and death,
  and whichever one chooses, it will be given.
¹⁸For great is the wisdom of God;
  God is mighty in power and sees everything;
¹⁹God's eyes are on those who fear God,
  and God knows every human deed,
²⁰has not commanded any one to be ungodly,
  and has not given any one permission to sin.

---

*Addition to the text. See Appendix.

Lesson 2 ~ 1 Corinthians 2:6-13

Paul instructs the Corinthians in the wisdom that comes from the Spirit of God.

⁶Yet among the mature we do impart wisdom, although it is not a wisdom of this age or of the rulers of this age, who are doomed to pass away. ⁷But we impart a secret and hidden wisdom of God, which God decreed before the ages for our glorification. ⁸None of the rulers of this age understood this; for if they had, they would not have crucified the Sovereign□ of glory. ⁹But, as it is written,
"What no eye has seen, nor ear heard,
nor the human heart conceived,
what God has prepared for those who love God,"
¹⁰God has revealed to us through the Spirit. For the Spirit searches everything, even the depths of God. ¹¹For who knows another's thoughts except the spirit of the person, which is within that person? So also no one comprehends the thoughts of God except the Spirit of God. ¹²Now we have received not the spirit of the world, but the Spirit which is from God, that we might understand the gifts bestowed on us by God. ¹³And we impart this in words not taught by human wisdom but taught by the Spirit, interpreting spiritual truths to those who possess the Spirit.

Gospel ~ Matthew 5:21-37

Jesus describes the righteousness of the realm of heaven.

²¹You have heard that it was said in ancient times, "You shall not kill; and whoever kills shall be liable to judgment." ²²But I say to you that every one who is angry with a neighbor** shall be liable to judgment; whoever insults a neighbor shall be liable to the council, and whoever says, "You fool!" shall be liable to the hell of fire. ²³So if you are offering your gift at the altar, and there remember that your neighbor has something against you, ²⁴leave your gift there before the altar and go; first be reconciled to your neighbor, and then come and offer your gift. ²⁵Make friends quickly with your accuser, while you are going to court, lest your accuser hand you over to the judge, and the judge to the guard, and you be put in prison; ²⁶truly, I say to you, you will never get out till you have paid the last penny.

□RSV *Lord.* See Appendix.
**In Matthew, especially in the Sermon on the Mount, *brother* is rendered *neighbor* in this lectionary. See Appendix.

²⁷You have heard that it was said, "You shall not commit adultery." ²⁸But I say to you that any one of you who looks at another lustfully has already committed adultery in your heart. ²⁹If your right eye causes you to sin, pluck it out and throw it away; it is better that you lose one of your members than that your whole body be thrown into hell. ³⁰And if your right hand causes you to sin, cut it off and throw it away; it is better that you lose one of your members than that your whole body go into hell.

³¹It was also said, "Whoever divorces his wife, let him give her a certificate of divorce." ³²But I say to you that every one who divorces his wife, except on the ground of unchastity, makes her an adulteress; and whoever marries a divorced woman commits adultery.**

³³Again you have heard that it was said in ancient times, "You shall not swear falsely, but shall perform to the Sovereign□ what you have sworn." ³⁴But I say to you, Do not swear at all, either by heaven, for it is the throne of God, ³⁵or by the earth, for it is God's footstool, or by Jerusalem, for it is the city of the great Ruler.□ ³⁶And do not swear by your head, for you cannot make one hair white or black. ³⁷Let what you say be simply "Yes" or "No"; anything more than this comes from evil.

**This teaching about divorce needs to be understood against the background of laws concerning divorce in Jesus' day. According to those laws, only women could be divorced, and they could be set aside for little provocation. Thus Jesus' words, which sound harsh and restrictive to modern ears, would have had a liberating effect on women in Jesus' day. See J. Jeremias, *Jerusalem in the Time of Jesus* (Fortress Press, 1969), pp. 370-371.
□RSV *Lord*. See Appendix.
□RSV *King*. See Appendix.

EPIPHANY 7

Lesson 1 ~ Leviticus 19:1-2, 9-18

Moses learns that to know God is to do justice.

¹And GOD said to Moses, ²"Say to all the congregation of the people of Israel, You shall be holy; for I the SOVEREIGN ONE your God am holy. . . .

⁹"When you reap the harvest of your land, you shall not reap your field to its very border, neither shall you gather the gleanings after your harvest. ¹⁰And you shall not strip your vineyard bare, neither shall you gather the fallen grapes of your vineyard; you shall leave them for the poor and for the sojourner: I am the SOVEREIGN ONE your God.

¹¹"You shall not steal, nor deal falsely, nor lie to one another. ¹²And you shall not swear by my name falsely, and so profane the name of your God: I am the SOVEREIGN ONE.

¹³"You shall not oppress or rob your neighbor. The wages of a hired servant shall not remain with you all night until the morning. ¹⁴You shall not curse the deaf or put a stumbling block before the blind, but you shall fear your God: I am the SOVEREIGN ONE.

¹⁵"You shall do no injustice in judgment; you shall not be partial to the poor or defer to the great, but in righteousness shall you judge your neighbor. ¹⁶You shall not go up and down, as a slanderer among your people, and you shall not stand forth against the life of your neighbor: I am the SOVEREIGN ONE.

¹⁷"You shall not hate your neighbor in your heart, but you shall reason with your neighbor, lest you bear sin because of that neighbor. ¹⁸You shall not take vengeance or bear any grudge against any of your own people, but you shall love your neighbor as yourself: I am the SOVEREIGN ONE."

Lesson 2 ~ 1 Corinthians 3:10-11, 16-23

Paul writes to the Corinthians that those who are Christ's are truly strong and wise.

¹⁰According to the grace of God given to me, like an expert builder I laid a foundation, and another is building upon it. Let each one take care how it is built upon. ¹¹For no other foundation can any one lay than that which is laid, which is Jesus Christ. . . .

¹⁶Do you not know that you are God's temple and that God's Spirit dwells in you? ¹⁷If any one destroys God's temple, God will destroy that person. For God's temple is holy, and that temple you are.

¹⁸Let none deceive themselves. If any among you think that they are

wise in this age, let them become fools that they may become wise. ¹⁹For the wisdom of this world is folly with God. For it is written, "God catches the wise in their craftiness," ²⁰and again, "The Sovereign One⁰ knows that the thoughts of the wise are futile." ²¹So let no one boast of mere human beings. For all things are yours, ²²whether Paul or Apollos or Cephas or the world or life or death or the present or the future, all are yours; ²³and you are Christ's; and Christ is God's.

Gospel ~ Matthew 5:38-48

Jesus tells the disciples to be merciful as God is merciful.

³⁸You have heard that it was said, "An eye for an eye and a tooth for a tooth." ³⁹But I say to you, Do not resist one who is evil. But if any one strikes you on the right cheek, turn the other also; ⁴⁰and if any one would sue you and take your coat, give your cloak as well; ⁴¹and if any one forces you to go one mile, go two miles. ⁴²Give to the one who begs from you, and do not refuse any one who would borrow from you.

⁴³You have heard that it was said, "You shall love your neighbor and hate your enemy." ⁴⁴But I say to you, Love your enemies and pray for those who persecute you, ⁴⁵so that you may be children of [God] your [Mother and*] Father who is in heaven; for God makes the sun rise on the evil and on the good, and sends rain on the just and on the unjust. ⁴⁶For if you love those who love you, what reward have you? Do not even the tax collectors do the same? ⁴⁷And if you salute only your neighbors, what more are you doing than others? Do not even the Gentiles do the same? ⁴⁸You, therefore, must be perfect, as [God] your heavenly Father [and Mother*] is perfect.

⁰RSV *Lord.* See Appendix.
*Addition to the text. See "Metaphor" and "God the Father and Mother" in the Appendix.

EPIPHANY 8

Lesson 1 ~ Isaiah 49:8-18

The prophet Isaiah speaks of the faithfulness of the God of Israel.

⁸Thus says the SOVEREIGN ONE:
"In a time of favor I have answered you,
   in a day of salvation I have helped you;
I have kept you and given you
   as a covenant to the people,
to establish the land,
   to apportion the desolate heritages;
⁹saying to the prisoners, 'Come forth,'
   to those who are in dungeons, 'Appear.'
They shall feed along the ways,
   on all bare heights shall be their pasture;
¹⁰they shall not hunger or thirst,
   neither scorching wind nor sun shall smite them,
for the one who has pity on them will lead them,
   and by springs of water will guide them.
¹¹And I will make all my mountains a way,
   and my highways shall be raised up.
¹²Lo, these shall come from afar,
   and lo, these from the north and from the west,
   and these from the land of Syene."
¹³Sing for joy, O heavens, and exult, O earth;
   break forth, O mountains, into singing!
For GOD has comforted God's people,
   and will have compassion on those who are afflicted.
¹⁴But Zion said, "The SOVEREIGN ONE has forsaken me,
   my God has forgotten me."
¹⁵"Can a woman forget her sucking child,
   that she should have no compassion on the fruit of her womb?
Even these may forget,
   yet I will not forget you.
¹⁶Behold, I have graven you on the palms of my hands;
   your walls are continually before me.
¹⁷Your builders outstrip your destroyers,
   and those who laid you waste go forth from you.
¹⁸Lift up your eyes round about and see;
   they all gather, they come to you.
As I live, says the SOVEREIGN ONE,
   you shall put them all on as an ornament,
   you shall bind them on as a bride does."

Lesson 2 ~ 1 Corinthians 4:1-13

Paul has become a fool for Christ's sake, that we might become wise.

¹This is how one should regard us, as servants of Christ and stewards of the mysteries of God. ²Moreover it is required of stewards that they be found trustworthy. ³But with me it is a very small thing that I should be judged by you or by any human court. I do not even judge myself. ⁴I am not aware of anything against myself, but I am not thereby acquitted. It is the Sovereign□ who judges me. ⁵Therefore do not pronounce judgment before the time, before the Sovereign□ comes, who will bring to light the things now hidden and will disclose the purposes of the heart. Then all will receive their commendation from God.

⁶I have applied all this to myself and Apollos for your benefit, my friends, that you may learn by us not to go beyond what is written, that none of you may be puffed up in favor of one against another. ⁷For who sees anything different in you? What have you that you did not receive? If then you received it, why do you boast as if it were not a gift?

⁸Already you are filled! Already you have become rich! Without us you have become rulers!□ And would that you did reign, so that we might share the rule with you! ⁹For I think that God has exhibited us apostles as last of all, like those who are sentenced to death; because we have become a spectacle to the world, to angels and to human beings. ¹⁰We are fools for Christ's sake, but you are wise in Christ. We are weak, but you are strong. You are held in honor, but we in disrepute. ¹¹To the present hour we hunger and thirst, we are ill-clad and buffeted and homeless, ¹²and we labor, working with our own hands. When reviled, we bless; when persecuted, we endure; ¹³when slandered, we try to conciliate; we have become, and are now, as the refuse of the world, the offscouring of all things.

□RSV *Lord*. See Appendix.
□RSV *kings*. See Appendix.

Gospel ~ Matthew 6:24-34

Jesus teaches the disciples to trust in God.

²⁴No one can serve two sovereigns;□ for either you will hate the one and love the other, or you will be devoted to the one and despise the other. You cannot serve God and mammon.

²⁵Therefore I tell you, do not be anxious about your life, what you shall eat or what you shall drink, nor about your body, what you shall put on. Is not life more than food, and the body more than clothing? ²⁶Look at the birds of the air: they neither sow nor reap nor gather into barns, and yet [God] your heavenly Father [and Mother*] feeds them. Are you not of more value than they? ²⁷And which of you by being anxious can add one cubit to your span of life? ²⁸And why are you anxious about clothing? Consider the lilies of the field, how they grow; they neither toil nor spin; ²⁹yet I tell you, even Solomon in all his glory was not arrayed like one of these. ³⁰But if God so clothes the grass of the field, which today is alive and tomorrow is thrown into the oven, will God not much more clothe you, O you of little faith? ³¹Therefore do not be anxious, saying, "What shall we eat?" or "What shall we drink?" or "What shall we wear?" ³²For the Gentiles seek all these things; and [God] your heavenly [Mother and*] Father knows that you need them all. ³³But seek first God's realm* and God's righteousness, and all these things shall be yours as well.

³⁴Therefore do not be anxious about tomorrow, for tomorrow will be anxious for itself. Let the day's own trouble be sufficient for the day.

□RSV *masters.*

*Addition to the text. See "Metaphor" and "God the Father and Mother" in the Appendix.

*RSV *kingdom.* See Appendix.

EPIPHANY 9

Lesson 1 ~ Exodus 24:12-18

Moses comes to God on the mountain.

[12]God said to Moses, "Come up to me on the mountain, and wait there; and I will give you the tables of stone, with the law and the commandment, which I have written for their instruction." [13]So Moses rose with his servant Joshua, and Moses went up into the mountain of God. [14]And Moses said to the elders, "Tarry here for us, until we come to you again; and, behold, Aaron and Hur are with you; whoever has a cause should go to them."

[15]Then Moses went up on the mountain, and the cloud covered the mountain. [16]The glory of God settled on Mount Sinai, and the cloud covered it six days; and on the seventh day God called to Moses out of the midst of the cloud. [17]Now the appearance of the glory of God was like a devouring fire on the top of the mountain in the sight of the people of Israel. [18]And Moses entered the cloud, and went up on the mountain. And Moses was on the mountain forty days and forty nights.

Lesson 2 ~ 2 Peter 1:16-21

True prophecy comes not from myths but from the Holy Spirit.

[16]For we did not follow cleverly devised myths when we made known to you the power and coming of our Sovereign□ Jesus Christ, but we were eyewitnesses of the Sovereign's majesty. [17]For when Christ Jesus received honor and glory from God the [*Mother and**] Father and the voice was borne to Christ by the Majestic Glory, "This is my beloved Child,◇ with whom I am well pleased," [18]we heard this voice borne from heaven, for we were with Christ on the holy mountain. [19]And we have the prophetic word made more sure. You will do well to pay attention to this as to a lamp shining in a dark place, until the day dawns and the morning star rises in your hearts. [20]First of all you must understand this, that no prophecy of scripture is a matter of one's own interpretation, [21]because no prophecy ever came by the human impulse, but people moved by the Holy Spirit spoke from God.

□RSV *Lord.* See Appendix.
*Addition to the text. See "Metaphor" and "God the Father and Mother" in the Appendix.
◇RSV *Son.* See Appendix.

In the presence of three disciples, Jesus is transfigured.

¹And after six days Jesus took Peter and James and John his brother, and led them up a high mountain apart. ²And Jesus was transfigured before them, and his face shone like the sun, and his garments became white as light. ³And behold, there appeared to them Moses and Elijah, talking with Jesus. ⁴And Peter said to Jesus, "My Sovereign,□ it is well that we are here; if you wish, I will make three booths here, one for you and one for Moses and one for Elijah." ⁵Peter was still speaking, when lo, a bright cloud overshadowed them, and a voice from the cloud said, "This is my beloved Child,◇ with whom I am well pleased; to this one you shall listen." ⁶When the disciples heard this, they fell on their faces, and were filled with awe. ⁷But Jesus came and touched them, saying, "Rise, and have no fear." ⁸And when they lifted up their eyes, they saw no one but Jesus only.

⁹And as they were coming down the mountain, Jesus commanded them, "Tell no one the vision, until the Human One○ is raised from the dead."

□RSV *Lord.* See Appendix.
◇RSV *Son.* See Appendix.
○RSV *Son of man.* See Appendix.

ASH WEDNESDAY

Lesson 1 ~ Joel 2:12-19

God calls the people to fasting and repentance.

12"Yet even now," says the SOVEREIGN ONE,
  "return to me with all your heart,
with fasting, with weeping, and with mourning;
13 and rend your hearts and not your garments."
 Return to the SOVEREIGN ONE, your God,
  for God is gracious and merciful,
 slow to anger, and abounding in steadfast love,
  and repents of evil.
14Who knows whether God will not turn and repent,
  and leave a blessing behind,
 a cereal offering and a drink offering
  for the SOVEREIGN ONE, your God?
15Blow the trumpet in Zion;
  sanctify a fast;
 call a solemn assembly;
16 gather the people.
 Sanctify the congregation;
  assemble the elders;
 gather the children,
  even nursing infants.
 Let the bridegroom leave his room,
  and the bride her chamber.
17Between the vestibule and the altar
  let the priests, the ministers of GOD, weep
 and say, "Spare your people, O SOVEREIGN ONE,
  and make not your heritage a reproach,
  a byword among the nations.
 Why should they say among the peoples,
  'Where is their God?' "
18Then GOD became jealous for the land,
  and had pity on God's people.
19GOD answered and said to the people,
  "Behold, I am sending to you
   grain, wine, and oil,
   and you will be satisfied;
 and I will no more make you
  a reproach among the nations."

Lesson 2 ~ 2 Corinthians 5:20b–6:10

Paul writes to the Corinthians of his ministry of reconciliation.

[20]We beseech you on behalf of Christ, be reconciled to God. [21]For our sake God made Christ to be sin who knew no sin, so that in Christ we might become the righteousness of God.
   [6:1]Working together with God, then, we entreat you not to accept the grace of God in vain. [2]For God says,
   "At the acceptable time I have listened to you,
   and helped you on the day of salvation."
Behold, now is the acceptable time; behold, now is the day of salvation. [3]We put no obstacle in any one's way, so that no fault may be found with our ministry, [4]but as servants of God we commend ourselves in every way: through great endurance, in afflictions, hardships, calamities, [5]beatings, imprisonments, tumults, labors, watching, hunger; [6]by purity, knowledge, forbearance, kindness, the Holy Spirit, genuine love, [7]truthful speech, and the power of God; with the weapons of righteousness for the right hand and for the left; [8]in honor and dishonor, in ill repute and good repute. We are treated as impostors, and yet are true; [9]as unknown, and yet well known; as dying, and behold we live; as punished, and yet not killed; [10]as sorrowful, yet always rejoicing; as poor, yet making many rich; as having nothing, and yet possessing everything.

Gospel ~ Matthew 6:1-6, 16-21

Jesus teaches the disciples to lay up treasure in heaven.

[1]Beware of practicing your piety before others in order to be seen by them; for then you will have no reward from [God] your Father [and Mother*] who is in heaven.
   [2]Thus, when you give alms, sound no trumpet before you, as the hypocrites do in the synagogues and in the streets, that they may be praised by others. Truly, I say to you, they have received their reward. [3]But when you give alms, do not let your left hand know what your right hand is doing, [4]so that your alms may be in secret; and God who sees in secret will reward you.
   [5]And when you pray, you must not be like the hypocrites; for they love to stand and pray in the synagogues and at the street corners, that they may be seen by others. Truly, I say to you, they have received their reward.

---

*Addition to the text. See "Metaphor" and "God the Father and Mother" in the Appendix.

⁶But when you pray, go into your room and shut the door and pray to God who is in secret; and God who sees in secret will reward you. . . .

¹⁶And when you fast, do not look dismal, like the hypocrites, for they disfigure their faces that their fasting may be seen by others. Truly, I say to you, they have received their reward. ¹⁷But when you fast, anoint your head and wash your face, ¹⁸that your fasting may not be seen by others but by God who is in secret; and God who sees in secret will reward you.

¹⁹Do not lay up for yourselves treasures on earth, where moth and rust consume and where thieves break in and steal, ²⁰but lay up for yourselves treasures in heaven, where neither moth nor rust consumes and where thieves do not break in and steal. ²¹For where your treasure is, there will your heart be also.

LENT 1

Lesson 1 ~ Genesis 2:4b-9, 15-18, 21-25; 3:1-7

God creates humankind.

[4]In the day that God the Sovereign One made the earth and the heavens, [5]when no plant of the field was yet in the earth and no herb of the field had yet sprung up—for the Sovereign One had not caused it to rain upon the earth, and there was no one to till the ground; [6]but a mist went up from the earth and watered the whole face of the ground—[7]then God the Sovereign One formed a human creature** of dust from the ground, and breathed into the creature's nostrils the breath of life; and the human creature became a living being. [8]And God the Sovereign One planted a garden in Eden, in the east; and there God put the human being whom God had formed. [9]And out of the ground God the Sovereign One made to grow every tree that is pleasant to the sight and good for food, the tree of life also in the midst of the garden, and the tree of the knowledge of good and evil. . . .

[15]God the Sovereign One took and placed the human being in the garden of Eden to till it and keep it. [16]And God the Sovereign One commanded the human being, saying, "You may freely eat of every tree of the garden; [17]but of the tree of the knowledge of good and evil you shall not eat, for in the day that you eat of it you shall die."

[18]Then God the Sovereign One said, "It is not good that the human being should be alone; I will make a companion corresponding to the creature." . . . [21] So God the Sovereign One caused a deep sleep to fall upon the human being, and took a rib out of the sleeping human being and closed up the place with flesh; [22]and God the Sovereign One built the rib which God took from the human being into woman and brought her to the man. [23]Then the man said,

"This at last is bone of my bones
    and flesh of my flesh;
she shall be called Woman,
    because she was taken out of Man."***

[24]Therefore a man leaves his father and his mother and cleaves to his wife, and they become one flesh. [25]And the man and woman were both naked, and were not ashamed.

**Life begins with the creation of *ha-'adam*, in v. 7. This Hebrew word does not refer to a particular person, but to a human creature from the earth. The creation of sexuality—of male and female, man and woman—does not occur until vs. 21-24.

***This literary pun on "man" (ish) and "woman" (ishshah) intends to show relationship rather than biological origin. The relationship is one of equality: "bone of my bones and flesh of my flesh."

³:¹Now the serpent was more subtle than any other wild creature that God the Sᴏᴠᴇʀᴇɪɢɴ Oɴᴇ had made. The serpent said to the woman, "Did God say, 'You shall not eat of any tree of the garden'?" ²And the woman said to the serpent, "We may eat of the fruit of the trees of the garden; ³but God said, 'You shall not eat of the fruit of the tree which is in the midst of the garden, neither shall you touch it, lest you die.' " ⁴But the serpent said to the woman, "You will not die. ⁵For God knows that when you eat of it your eyes will be opened, and you will be like God, knowing good and evil." ⁶So when the woman saw that the tree was good for food, and that it was a delight to the eyes, and that the tree was to be desired to make one wise, she took of its fruit and ate; and she also gave some to her husband, and he ate. ⁷Then the eyes of both were opened, and they knew that they were naked; and they sewed fig leaves together and made themselves aprons.

Lesson 2 ～ Romans 5:12-21

Paul writes of the trespass of Adam and of the grace of Jesus Christ.

¹²Therefore as sin came into the world through one human being and death through sin, and so death spread to all humanity because all sinned—¹³sin indeed was in the world before the law was given, but sin is not counted where there is no law. ¹⁴Yet death reigned from Adam to Moses, even over those whose sins were not like the transgression of Adam, who was a type of the one who was to come.

¹⁵But the free gift is not like the trespass. For if many died through the trespass of one, much more have the grace of God and the free gift in the grace of that one person Jesus Christ abounded for many. ¹⁶And the free gift is not like the effect of that one's sin. For the judgment following one trespass brought condemnation, but the free gift following many trespasses brings justification. ¹⁷If, because of the trespass of one, death reigned through that one, much more will those who receive the abundance of grace and the free gift of righteousness reign in life through the one person Jesus Christ.

¹⁸Then as the trespass of one led to condemnation for all, so the act of righteousness of one leads to acquittal and life for all. ¹⁹For as by the disobedience of one many were made sinners, so by the obedience of one many will be made righteous. ²⁰Law came in, to increase the trespass; but where sin increased, grace abounded all the more, ²¹so that, as sin reigned in death, grace also might reign through righteousness to eternal life through our Sovereign▫ Jesus Christ.

▫RSV *Lord*. See Appendix.

Jesus is tempted by the devil.

¹Then Jesus was led up by the Spirit into the wilderness to be tempted by the devil. ²Having fasted forty days and forty nights, Jesus was hungry. ³And the tempter came and said to Jesus, "If you are the Child* of God, command these stones to become loaves of bread." ⁴But Jesus answered, "It is written,

'One shall not live by bread alone,

but by every word that proceeds from the mouth of God.'"

⁵Then the devil took Jesus to the holy city, and set him on the pinnacle of the temple, ⁶and said, "If you are the Child* of God, throw yourself down; for it is written,

'God will give the angels charge of you,'

and

'On their hands they will bear you up,

lest you strike your foot against a stone.'"

⁷Jesus said to the devil, "Again it is written, 'You shall not tempt the Sovereign One your God.'" ⁸Again, the devil took Jesus to a very high mountain, and showed him all the nations of the world and the glory of them; ⁹and the devil said to Jesus, "All these I will give you, if you will fall down and worship me." ¹⁰Then Jesus said to the devil, "Begone, Satan! for it is written,

'You shall worship the Sovereign One your God,

and God only shall you serve.' "

¹¹Then the devil left Jesus, and behold, angels came and ministered to him.

---

*RSV *Son.* See Appendix.

LENT 2

Lesson 1 ~ Genesis 12:1-8

Abram and Sarai are chosen to play a decisive role in God's purpose for history.

[1]Now GOD said to Abram, "Go from your country and your kindred and your family's house to the land that I will show you. [2]And I will make of you a great nation, and I will bless you, and make your name great, so that you will be a blessing. [3]I will bless those who bless you, and the one who curses you I will curse; and by you all the families of the earth shall bless themselves."
[4]So Abram went, as GOD had told him; and Lot went with him. Abram was seventy-five years old when he departed from Haran. [5]And Abram took Sarai his wife, and Lot his nephew, and all their possessions which they had gathered, and the persons that they had gotten in Haran; and they set forth to go to the land of Canaan. When they had come to the land of Canaan, [6]Abram passed through the land to the place at Shechem, to the oak of Moreh. At that time the Canaanites were in the land. [7]Then GOD appeared to Abram, and said, "To your descendants I will give this land." So Abram built there an altar to GOD, who had appeared to him. [8]Thence Abram removed to the mountain on the east of Bethel, and pitched a tent, with Bethel on the west and Ai on the east; and there Abram built an altar to GOD and called on the name of the SOVEREIGN ONE.

Lesson 2 ~ Romans 4:1-9, 13-17

The true descendants of Abraham and Sarah are those who have faith in Christ.

[1]What then shall we say about Abraham, our ancestor according to the flesh? [2]For if Abraham was justified by works, he has something to boast about, but not before God. [3]For what does the scripture say? "Abraham believed God, and it was reckoned to Abraham as righteousness." [4]Now to one who works, wages are not reckoned as a gift but as the worker's due. [5]And to one who does not work but trusts God who justifies the ungodly, faith is reckoned as righteousness. [6]So also David pronounces a blessing upon the person to whom God reckons righteousness apart from works:
[7]"Blessed are those whose iniquities are forgiven, and whose sins are covered;
[8]blessed are those against whom the Sovereign One□ will not reckon their sin."
[9]Is this blessing pronounced only upon the Jews, or also upon the Gentiles? We say that faith was reckoned to Abraham as righteousness. . . .

□RSV *Lord.* See Appendix.

¹³The promise to Abraham [*and Sarah**] and their descendants, that they should inherit the world, did not come through the law but through the righteousness of faith. ¹⁴If it is the adherents of the law who are to be the heirs, faith is null and the promise is void. ¹⁵For the law brings wrath, but where there is no law there is no transgression.

¹⁶That is why it depends on faith, in order that the promise may rest on grace and be guaranteed to all their descendants—not only to the adherents of the law but also to those who share the faith of Abraham [*and Sarah**], who are the ancestors of us all, ¹⁷as it is written, "I have made you the ancestors of many nations"—in the presence of the God in whom Abraham [*and Sarah**] believed, who gives life to the dead and calls into existence the things that do not exist.

Gospel ~ John 3:1-17

Nicodemus comes to Jesus to learn how to be born again.

¹Now there was a man of the Pharisees, named Nicodemus, a ruler of the Jews. ²Nicodemus came to Jesus by night and said to Jesus, "Rabbi, we know that you are a teacher come from God; for no one can do these signs that you do, except by the power of God." ³Jesus answered Nicodemus, "Truly, truly, I say to you, unless one is born anew,** one cannot see the realm* of God." ⁴Nicodemus replied, "How can someone be born who is old? Can one enter a second time the womb of one's mother and be born?" ⁵Jesus answered, "Truly, truly, I say to you, unless one is born of water and the Spirit, one cannot enter the realm* of God. ⁶That which is born of the flesh is flesh, and that which is born of the Spirit is spirit. ⁷Do not marvel that I said to you, 'You must be born anew.**' ⁸The wind blows where it wills, and you hear the sound of it, but you do not know whence it comes or whither it goes; so it is with every one who is born of the Spirit."⁹Nicodemus said to Jesus, "How can this be?" ¹⁰Jesus answered, "Are you a teacher of Israel, and yet you do not understand this? ¹¹Truly, truly, I say to you, we speak of what we know, and bear witness to what we have seen; but you do not receive our testimony. ¹²If I have told you earthly things and you do not believe, how can you believe if I tell you heavenly things? ¹³No one has ascended into heaven but the one who descended from heaven, the Human One.° ¹⁴And as Moses lifted up the serpent in the wilderness, so must the Human One° be lifted up, ¹⁵that whoever believes in that one may have eternal life."

¹⁶For God so loved the world that God gave God's only Child,◇ that whoever believes in that Child should not perish but have eternal life. ¹⁷For God sent that Child◇ into the world, not to condemn the world, but that through that Child the world might be saved.

---

*Addition to the text. See Appendix.   °RSV *Son of man.* See Appendix.
**Or *from above.*   ◇RSV v. 16 *Son;* v. 17 *the Son.* See Appendix.
*RSV *kingdom.* See Appendix.

LENT 3

Lesson 1 ~ Exodus 17:3-7

Moses brings water from a rock at Massah.

3But the people thirsted there for water, and the people murmured against Moses, and said, "Why did you bring us up out of Egypt, to kill us and our children and our cattle with thirst?" 4So Moses cried to GOD, "What shall I do with this people? They are almost ready to stone me." 5And GOD said to Moses, "Pass on before the people, taking with you some of the elders of Israel; and take in your hand the rod with which you struck the Nile, and go. 6Behold, I will stand before you there on the rock at Horeb; and you shall strike the rock, and water shall come out of it, that the people may drink." And Moses did so, in the sight of the elders of Israel. 7And he called the name of the place Massah and Meribah, because of the faultfinding of the children of Israel, and because they put GOD to the proof by saying, "Is GOD among us or not?"

Lesson 2 ~ Romans 5:1-11

Paul writes to the Roman church of the greatness of God's love.

1Therefore, since we are justified by faith, we have peace with God through our Sovereign□ Jesus Christ, 2 through whom we have obtained access to this grace in which we stand, and we rejoice in our hope of sharing the glory of God. 3More than that, we rejoice in our sufferings, knowing that suffering produces endurance, 4and endurance produces character, and character produces hope, 5and hope does not disappoint us, because God's love has been poured into our hearts through the Holy Spirit which has been given to us.
6While we were still weak, at the right time Christ died for the ungodly. 7Why, one will hardly die for a righteous person—though perhaps for good people one will dare even to die. 8But God shows love for us in that while we were yet sinners Christ died for us. 9Since, therefore, we are now justified by the blood of Christ, much more shall we be saved by Christ from the wrath of God. 10For if while we were enemies we were reconciled to God by the death of God's Child,◇ much more, now that we are reconciled, shall we be saved by the life of Christ. 11Not only so, but we also rejoice in God through our Sovereign□ Jesus Christ, through whom we have now received our reconciliation.

□RSV *Lord.* See Appendix.
◇RSV *Son.* See Appendix.

This is the story of Jesus' encounter with the woman at the well in Samaria.

⁵So Jesus came to a city of Samaria, called Sychar, near the field that Jacob gave to his son Joseph. ⁶Jacob's well was there, and so Jesus, wearied with the journey, sat down beside the well. It was about the sixth hour.

⁷There came a woman of Samaria to draw water. Jesus said to her, "Give me a drink." ⁸For the disciples had gone away into the city to buy food. ⁹The Samaritan woman said to Jesus, "How is it that you, a Jew, ask a drink of me, a woman of Samaria?" For Jews have no dealings with Samaritans. ¹⁰Jesus answered her, "If you knew the gift of God, and who it is that is saying to you, 'Give me a drink,' you would have asked that person, and that one would have given you living water." ¹¹The woman said to Jesus, "You have nothing to draw with, and the well is deep; where do you get that living water? ¹²Are you greater than our ancestor Jacob, who gave us the well, and drank from it, as did his children and cattle?" ¹³Jesus said to her, "Every one who drinks of this water will thirst again, ¹⁴but whoever drinks of the water that I shall give will never thirst; the water that I shall give will become in the one who drinks it a spring of water welling up to eternal life." ¹⁵The woman said to Jesus, "Give me this water, that I may not thirst, nor come here to draw."

¹⁶Jesus said to her, "Go, call your husband, and come here." ¹⁷The woman answered, "I have no husband." Jesus said to her, "You are right in saying, 'I have no husband'; ¹⁸for you have had five husbands, and he whom you now have is not your husband; this you said truly." ¹⁹The woman said to Jesus, "I perceive that you are a prophet. ²⁰Our ancestors worshiped on this mountain; and you say that in Jerusalem is the place where people ought to worship." ²¹Jesus said to her, "Woman, believe me, the hour is coming when neither on this mountain nor in Jerusalem will you worship [*God*] the Father [*and Mother**]. ²²You worship what you do not know; we worship what we know, for salvation is from the Jews. ²³But the hour is coming, and now is, when the true worshipers will worship [*God*] the [*Mother and**] Father in spirit and truth, for such are the ones God seeks as worshipers. ²⁴God is spirit, and those who worship God must worship in spirit and truth." ²⁵The woman said to Jesus, "I know that Messiah is coming (the one who is called Christ), who, having come, will show us all things." ²⁶Jesus said to her, "I who speak to you am that very one."

²⁷Just then the disciples came. They marveled that Jesus was talking with a woman, but none said, "What do you wish?" or, "Why are you talking with her?" ²⁸So the woman left her water jar, and went away into the

---

*Addition to the text. See "Metaphor" and "God the Father and Mother" in the Appendix.

city, and said to the people, ²⁹"Come, see the one who told me all that I ever did. Can this be the Christ?" ³⁰They went out of the city and were coming to Jesus.

³¹Meanwhile the disciples besought Jesus, saying, "Rabbi, eat." ³²But Jesus said to them, "I have food to eat of which you do not know." ³³So the disciples said to one another, "Has any one brought Jesus food?" ³⁴Jesus said to them, "My food is to do the will of God who sent me, and to accomplish God's work. ³⁵Do you not say, 'There are yet four months, then comes the harvest'? I tell you, lift up your eyes, and see how the fields are already white for harvest. ³⁶One who reaps receives wages, and gathers fruit for eternal life, so that sower and reaper may rejoice together. ³⁷For here the saying holds true, 'One sows and another reaps.' ³⁸I sent you to reap that for which you did not labor; others have labored, and you have entered into their labor."

³⁹Many Samaritans from that city believed in Jesus because of the woman's testimony, "This person told me all that I ever did." ⁴⁰So when the Samaritans approached, they asked Jesus to stay with them; and he stayed there two days. ⁴¹And many more believed because of Jesus' word. ⁴²They said to the woman, "It is no longer because of your words that we believe, for we have heard for ourselves, and we know that this is indeed the Savior of the world."

LENT 4

Lesson 1 ~ 1 Samuel 16:1-18

Samuel anoints David as king over Israel.

¹GOD said to Samuel, "How long will you grieve over Saul, seeing I have rejected him from being king over Israel? Fill your horn with oil, and go; I will send you to Jesse the Bethlehemite, for I have provided for myself a king among Jesse's sons." ²And Samuel said, "How can I go? If Saul hears it, he will kill me." And GOD said, "Take a heifer with you, and say, 'I have come to sacrifice to GOD.' ³And invite Jesse to the sacrifice, and I will show you what you shall do; and you shall anoint for me the one whom I name to you." ⁴Samuel did what GOD commanded, and came to Bethlehem. The elders of the city came to meet Samuel trembling, and said, "Do you come peaceably?" ⁵And Samuel said, "Peaceably; I have come to sacrifice to GOD; consecrate yourselves, and come with me to the sacrifice." And he consecrated Jesse and his sons, and invited them to the sacrifice.

⁶When they came, Samuel looked on Eliab and thought, "Surely GOD's anointed is present." ⁷But GOD said to Samuel, "Do not look on Eliab's appearance or on the height of his stature, because I have rejected Eliab; for GOD sees not as people see; people look on the outward appearance, but GOD looks on the heart." ⁸Then Jesse called Abinadab, and made Abinadab pass before Samuel. And Samuel said, "Neither has GOD chosen this one." ⁹Then Jesse made Shammah pass by. And Samuel said, "Neither has GOD chosen this one." ¹⁰And Jesse made seven of his sons pass before Samuel. And Samuel said to Jesse, "GOD has not chosen these." ¹¹And Samuel said to Jesse, "Are all your sons here?" And Jesse said, "There remains yet the youngest, but behold, that one is keeping the sheep." And Samuel said to Jesse, "Send and fetch him; for we will not sit down till he comes here." ¹²And Jesse sent, and brought David in. Now David was ruddy, and had beautiful eyes, and was handsome. And GOD said, "Arise, anoint David; for this is the one." ¹³Then Samuel took the horn of oil, and anointed David in the midst of his brothers; and the Spirit of GOD came mightily upon David from that day forward. And Samuel rose up, and went to Ramah.

¹⁴Now the Spirit of GOD departed from Saul, and an evil spirit from GOD tormented Saul. ¹⁵And Saul's servants said to him, "Behold now, an evil spirit from God is tormenting you. ¹⁶Let our lord now command your servants, who are before you, to seek out someone who is skilful in playing the lyre; and when the evil spirit from God is upon you, that person will play it, and you will be well." ¹⁷So Saul said to the servants, "Provide for me someone who can play well, and bring that person to me." ¹⁸One of the young servants answered, "Behold, I have seen a son of Jesse the Bethlehemite, who is skilful in playing, a person of valor, a warrior, prudent in speech, and of good presence; and GOD is with him."

Lesson 2 ~ Ephesians 5:8-14

The Ephesians learn to walk as children of light.

⁸For once you were stumbling in the night, but now you are light in the Sovereign;□ walk as children of light ⁹(for the fruit of light is found in all that is good and right and true), ¹⁰and try to learn what is pleasing to the Sovereign.□ ¹¹Take no part in unfruitful works, but instead expose them. ¹²For it is a shame even to speak of the things that are done in secret; ¹³but when anything is exposed by the light it becomes visible, for anything that becomes visible is light. ¹⁴Therefore it is said,

"Awake, O sleeper, and arise from the dead,
and Christ shall give you light."

Gospel ~ John 9:1-41**

Jesus heals the one born blind.

¹As Jesus passed by, he saw a person blind from birth. ²And the disciples asked Jesus, "Rabbi, who sinned, this person or the parents, that the child was born blind?" ³Jesus answered, "It was not that this person sinned, or the parents, but that the works of God might be made manifest. ⁴We must work the works of the one who sent me, while it is day; night comes, when no one can work. ⁵As long as I am in the world, I am the light of the world." ⁶As Jesus said this, he spat on the ground and made clay of the spittle and anointed the blind person's eyes with the clay, ⁷saying, "Go, wash in the pool of Siloam" (which means Sent). So the blind person went and washed and came back seeing. ⁸The neighbors and those who had seen the person before as a beggar, said, "Is not this the one who used to sit and beg?" ⁹Some said, "It is the one"; others said, "No, but they look alike." The one born blind said, "I am that person." ¹⁰They said, "Then how were your eyes opened?" ¹¹The answer came, "The one called Jesus made clay and anointed my eyes and said to me, 'Go to Siloam and wash'; so I went and washed and received my sight." ¹²They asked, "Where is Jesus?" The one born blind said, "I do not know." ¹³They brought to the Pharisees the one who had formerly been blind. ¹⁴Now it was a sabbath day when Jesus made the clay and opened the blind one's eyes. ¹⁵The Pharisees again asked that person how sight had been restored. And the person said to them, "He put clay on my eyes, and I washed, and I see." ¹⁶Some of the Pharisees said, "This one is not from God, for he does not keep the sabbath." But others said, "How can a person who is a sinner do such signs?" There was a division

---

□RSV *Lord.* See Appendix.
**Because the one born blind is never identified by name, masculine pronouns have been omitted in order to invite women as well as men to hear their condition addressed in this passage.

among them. [17]So they again said to the blind person, "What do you say about Jesus, since he has opened your eyes?" The blind person said, "Jesus is a prophet."

[18]The Jews did not believe that the person had been blind and had received sight, until they called the parents of the one who had received sight, [19]and asked them, "Is this your child, who you say was born blind? How then does this one now see?" [20]The parents answered, "We know that this is our child, who was born blind; [21]but how our child now sees we do not know, nor do we know who opened those blind eyes. Ask the one born blind, who is of age and will speak directly." [22]The parents said this because they feared the leaders of the Jews, for the leaders had already agreed that any one who confessed Jesus to be Christ would be put out of the synagogue. [23]Therefore the parents said, "Our child is of age, ask the child." [24]So for the second time they called the one who had been blind, and said, "Give God the praise; we know that this Jesus is a sinner." [25]The one born blind answered, "Whether Jesus is a sinner, I do not know; one thing I know, that though I was blind, now I see." [26]They said, "What did Jesus do to you? How did Jesus open your eyes?" [27]The one born blind answered them, "I have told you already, and you would not listen. Why do you want to hear it again? Do you too want to become Jesus' disciples?" [28]And they reviled the one born blind, saying, "You are Jesus' disciple, but we are disciples of Moses. [29]We know that God has spoken to Moses, but as for this Jesus, we do not know where he comes from." [30]The one born blind answered, "Why, this is a marvel! You do not know where Jesus comes from, and yet he opened my eyes. [31]We know that God does not listen to sinners, but if any one is a worshiper of God and does God's will, God listens. [32]Never since the world began has it been heard that any one opened the eyes of someone born blind. [33]If this Jesus were not from God, he could do nothing." [34]They answered, "You were born in utter sin, and would you teach us?" And they cast out the one born blind.

[35]Jesus heard that they had cast that one out, and having found the one born blind, Jesus said, "Do you believe in the Human One?"[o] [36]The one born blind answered, "And who is that, so that I may believe in whoever it is?" [37]Jesus said, "You have seen who it is, and it is the very one who speaks to you." [38]The one born blind said, "My Sovereign,[□] I believe"; and worshiped Jesus. [39]Jesus said, "For judgment I came into this world, that those who do not see may see, and that those who see may become blind." [40]Some of the Pharisees nearby heard this, and they said to Jesus, "Are we also blind?" [41]Jesus said to them, "If you were blind, you would have no guilt; but now that you say, 'We see,' your guilt remains."

---

[o]RSV *Son of man.* See Appendix.
[□]RSV *Lord.* See Appendix.

LENT 5

Lesson 1 ~ Ezekiel 37:1-14

A vision of the valley of the dry bones is given to Ezekiel.

¹The hand of GOD was upon me, and brought me out by the Spirit of GOD, and set me down in the midst of the valley; it was full of bones. ²And God led me round among them; and behold, there were very many upon the valley; and lo, they were very dry. ³And God said to me, "O mortal,** can these bones live?" And I answered, "O Sovereign GOD, you know." ⁴Again God said to me, "Prophesy to these bones, and say to them, O dry bones, hear the word of GOD. ⁵Thus says the Sovereign GOD to these bones: Behold, I will cause breath to enter you, and you shall live. ⁶And I will lay sinews upon you, and will cause flesh to come upon you, and cover you with skin, and put breath in you, and you shall live; and you shall know that I am the SOVEREIGN ONE."

⁷So I prophesied as I was commanded; and as I prophesied, there was a noise, and behold, a rattling; and the bones came together, bone to its bone. ⁸And as I looked, there were sinews on them, and flesh had come upon them, and skin had covered them; but there was no breath in them. ⁹Then God said to me, "Prophesy to the breath, prophesy, O mortal,** and say to the breath, Thus says the Sovereign GOD: Come from the four winds, O breath, and breathe upon these slain, that they may live." ¹⁰So I prophesied as God commanded me, and the breath came into them, and they lived, and stood upon their feet, an exceedingly great host.

¹¹Then God said to me, "O mortal,** these bones are the whole house of Israel. Behold, they say, 'Our bones are dried up, and our hope is lost; we are clean cut off.' ¹²Therefore prophesy, and say to them, Thus says the Sovereign GOD: Behold, I will open your graves, and raise you from your graves, O my people; and I will bring you home into the land of Israel. ¹³And you shall know that I am the SOVEREIGN ONE, when I open your graves, and raise you from your graves, O my people. ¹⁴And I will put my Spirit within you, and you shall live, and I will place you in your own land; then you shall know that I, the SOVEREIGN ONE, have spoken, and I have done it, says GOD."

Lesson 2 ~ Romans 8:6-19

Paul describes to the Romans the life in the Spirit.

⁶To set the mind on the flesh is death, but to set the mind on the Spirit is life and peace. ⁷For the mind that is set on the flesh is hostile to God; it does not submit to God's law, indeed it cannot; ⁸and those who are in the flesh cannot please God.

**RSV vs. 3, 11 *Son of man;* v. 9 *son of man.*

⁹But you are not in the flesh, you are in the Spirit, if in fact the Spirit of God dwells in you. Any one who does not have the Spirit of Christ does not belong to Christ. ¹⁰But if Christ is in you, although your bodies are dead because of sin, your spirits are alive because of righteousness. ¹¹If the Spirit of the one who raised Jesus from the dead dwells in you, the one who raised Christ Jesus from the dead will give life to your mortal bodies also through that Spirit which dwells in you.

¹²So then, brothers and sisters, we are debtors, not to the flesh, to live according to the flesh—¹³for if you live according to the flesh you will die, but if by the Spirit you put to death the deeds of the body you will live. ¹⁴For all who are led by the Spirit of God are children of God. ¹⁵For you did not receive the spirit of slavery to fall back into fear, but you have received the spirit of adoption as heirs. When we cry, "[*God! my Mother and***]Father!*" ¹⁶it is the Spirit bearing witness with our spirit that we are children of God, ¹⁷and if children, then heirs, heirs of God and joint heirs with Christ, provided we suffer with Christ in order that we may also be glorified with Christ.

¹⁸I consider that the sufferings of this present time are not worth comparing with the glory that is to be revealed to us. ¹⁹For the creation waits with eager longing for the revealing of the children of God.

Gospel ~ John 11:1-53

Jesus raises Lazarus from the dead.

¹Now a certain person was ill, Lazarus of Bethany, the village of Mary and her sister Martha. ²It was Mary who anointed the Sovereign□ with ointment and wiped his feet with her hair, whose brother Lazarus was ill. ³So the sisters sent to Jesus, saying, "The one you love is ill." ⁴But hearing it, Jesus said, "This illness is not unto death; it is for the glory of God, so that the Child◇ of God may be glorified by means of it."

⁵Now Jesus loved Martha and her sister Mary, and Lazarus. ⁶And hearing that Lazarus was ill, Jesus stayed two days longer in the place where he was. ⁷Then after this Jesus said to the disciples, "Let us go into Judea again." ⁸The disciples replied, "Rabbi, the Jews were but now seeking to stone you, and are you going there again?" ⁹Jesus answered, "Are there not twelve hours in the day? Those who walk in the day do not stumble, because they see the light of this world. ¹⁰But those who walk in

---

Abba! Father! The word *"Abba!"* is an intimate form, and Jesus' use of this term to refer to God was radically nontraditional. This warrants the use of nontraditional intimate language in contemporary reference to God. See also Gal. 4:6 (Christmas 1, Lesson 2). □RSV *Lord*. See Appendix. ◇RSV *Son*. See Appendix.

the night stumble, because the light is not in them." [11]Thus Jesus spoke to the disciples, and then added, "Our friend Lazarus has fallen asleep, but I go to awake him out of sleep." [12]The disciples said to Jesus, "If he has fallen asleep, he will recover." [13]Now Jesus had spoken of the death of Lazarus, but they thought that he meant taking rest in sleep. [14]Then Jesus told them plainly, "Lazarus is dead; [15]and for your sake I am glad I was not there, so that you may believe. But let us go to him." [16]Thomas, called the Twin, said to the other disciples, "Let us also go, that we may die with him."

[17]Now when Jesus came, he found that Lazarus had already been in the tomb four days. [18]Bethany was near Jerusalem, about two miles off, [19]and many of the Jews had come to Martha and Mary to console them concerning their brother. [20]When Martha heard that Jesus was coming, she went and met him, while Mary sat in the house. [21]Martha said to Jesus, "If you had been here, my brother would not have died. [22]And even now I know that whatever you ask from God, God will give you." [23]Jesus said to her, "Your brother will rise again." [24]Martha said to Jesus, "I know that Lazarus will rise again in the resurrection at the last day." [25]Jesus said to her, "I am the resurrection and the life; those who believe in me, though they die, yet shall they live, [26]and whoever lives and believes in me shall never die. Do you believe this?" [27]She said to Jesus, "Yes, I believe that you are the Christ, the Child° of God, the one who is coming into the world."

[28]When Martha had said this, she went and called her sister Mary, saying quietly, "The Teacher is here and is calling for you." [29]And when Mary heard it, she rose quickly and went to Jesus. [30]Now Jesus had not yet come to the village, but was still in the place where Martha had met him. [31]When the Jews who were with her in the house, consoling her, saw Mary rise quickly and go out, they followed her, supposing that she was going to the tomb to weep there. [32]Then Mary came and saw Jesus, fell at Jesus' feet, and said, "If you had been here, my brother would not have died." [33]When Jesus saw her weeping, and the Jews who came with her also weeping, Jesus was deeply moved in spirit and troubled, [34]and said, "Where have you laid Lazarus?" They said to Jesus, "Come and see." [35]Jesus wept. [36]So the Jews said, "See how Jesus loved Lazarus!" [37]But some of them said, "Could not the one who opened the eyes of the blind have kept this one from dying?"

[38]Then Jesus, deeply moved again, came to the tomb; it was a cave, and a stone lay upon it. [39]Jesus said, "Take away the stone." Martha, the sister of the dead Lazarus, said to Jesus, "By this time there will be an odor, for my brother has been dead four days." [40]Jesus said to her, "Did I not tell you that if you would believe you would see the glory of God?" [41]So they took away the stone. And Jesus looked up and said, "[*God, my Mother and**]

Father, I thank you that you have heard me. ⁴²I knew that you hear me always, but I have said this on account of the people standing by, that they may believe that you sent me." ⁴³Having said this, Jesus cried with a loud voice, "Lazarus, come out." ⁴⁴The dead man came out, hands and feet bound with bandages, and face wrapped with a cloth. Jesus said to them, "Unbind Lazarus, and let him go."

⁴⁵Many of the Jews therefore, who had come with Mary and had seen what was done, believed in Jesus; ⁴⁶but some of them went to the Pharisees and told them what Jesus had done. ⁴⁷So the chief priests and the Pharisees gathered the council, and said, "What are we to do? For this one performs many signs. ⁴⁸If we do not interfere, every one will believe in Jesus, and the Romans will come and destroy both our holy place and our nation." ⁴⁹But one of them, Caiaphas, who was high priest that year, said to them, "You know nothing at all; ⁵⁰you do not understand that it is expedient for you that one person should die for the people, and that the whole nation should not perish." ⁵¹Caiaphas did not say this of his own accord, but being high priest that year, prophesied that Jesus should die for the nation, ⁵²and not for the nation only, but to gather into one the children of God who are scattered abroad. ⁵³So from that day on they took counsel how to put Jesus to death.

PASSION SUNDAY

Lesson 1 ~ Isaiah 50:4-9a

The prophet Isaiah tells of the suffering of the disciple of God.

4The Sovereign GOD has given me
  the tongue of those who are taught,
that I may know how to sustain with a word
  one who is weary.
Morning by morning God wakens,
  God wakens my ear
to hear as those who are taught.
5The Sovereign GOD has opened my ear,
  and I was not rebellious,
  I turned not backward.
6I gave my back to the smiters,
  and my cheeks to those who pulled out the beard;
I hid not my face
  from shame and spitting.
7For the Sovereign GOD helps me;
  therefore I have not been confounded;
therefore I have set my face like a flint,
  and I know that I shall not be put to shame;
8 the one who vindicates me is near.
Who will contend with me?
  Let us stand together.
Who are my adversaries?
  Let them come near to me.
9Behold, the Sovereign GOD helps me;
  who will declare me guilty?

Lesson 2 ~ Philippians 2:5-11

Paul speaks about the sovereignty of Jesus Christ.

5Have this mind among yourselves, which is yours in Christ Jesus,
6who, though being in the form of God, did not count equality with God a
thing to be grasped, 7but emptied self, taking the form of a servant, being
born in the likeness of human beings. 8And being found in human form,
Christ humbled self and became obedient unto death, even death on a

cross. ⁹Therefore God has highly exalted Jesus and bestowed on Jesus the name which is above every name, ¹⁰that at the name of Jesus every knee should bow, in heaven and on earth and under the earth, ¹¹and every tongue confess that Jesus Christ is Sovereign,□ to the glory of God the Father [*and Mother**].

Gospel ~ Matthew 26:14–27:66

The passion of Jesus begins with the institution of the Last Supper.

¹⁴Then one of the twelve, who was called Judas Iscariot, went to the chief priests ¹⁵and said, "What will you give me if I deliver Jesus to you?" And they paid Judas thirty pieces of silver. ¹⁶And from that moment he sought an opportunity to betray Jesus.

¹⁷Now on the first day of Unleavened Bread the disciples came to Jesus, saying, "Where will you have us prepare for you to eat the passover?" ¹⁸Jesus replied, "Go into the city to a certain one, and say, 'The Teacher says, My time is at hand; I will keep the passover at your house with my disciples.' " ¹⁹And the disciples did as Jesus had directed them, and they prepared the passover.

²⁰When it was evening, Jesus sat at table with the twelve disciples, ²¹and as they were eating, said, "Truly, I say to you, one of you will betray me." ²²And they were very sorrowful, and began to say to Jesus one after another, "Is it I?" ²³Jesus answered, "The one who has dipped a hand in the dish with me, will betray me. ²⁴The Human One° goes as it is written, but woe to that person by whom the Human One° is betrayed! It would have been better for that one not to have been born." ²⁵Judas, who betrayed Jesus, said, "Is it I, Teacher?" Jesus said to him, "You have said so."

²⁶Now as they were eating, Jesus took bread, and blessed, and broke it, and gave it to the disciples and said, "Take, eat; this is my body." ²⁷Then taking a cup, and having given thanks, Jesus gave it to them, saying, "Drink of it, all of you; ²⁸for this is my blood of the covenant, which is poured out for many for the forgiveness of sins. ²⁹I tell you I shall not drink again of this fruit of the vine until that day when I drink it new with you in the realm* of God."

³⁰And when they had sung a hymn, they went out to the Mount of Olives. ³¹Then Jesus said to them, "You will all fall away because of me this night; for it is written, 'I will strike the shepherd, and the sheep of the flock will be scattered.' ³²But after I am raised up, I will go before you to

---

□RSV *Lord.* See Appendix.
*Addition to the text. See "Metaphor" and "God the Father and Mother" in the Appendix.
°RSV *Son of man.* See Appendix.
*RSV *kingdom.* See Appendix.

Galilee." ³³Peter declared to Jesus, "Though they all fall away because of you, I will never fall away." ³⁴Jesus said to him, "Truly, I say to you, this very night, before the cock crows, you will deny me three times." ³⁵Peter said to Jesus, "Even if I must die with you, I will not deny you." And so said all the disciples.

³⁶Then Jesus went with them to a place called Gethsemane, and said to the disciples, "Sit here, while I go yonder and pray." ³⁷And taking with him Peter and the two sons of Zebedee, Jesus began to be sorrowful and troubled. ³⁸Then Jesus said to them, "My soul is very sorrowful, even to death; remain here, and watch with me." ³⁹And going a little farther Jesus fell to the ground and prayed, "[God] my Father [and Mother*], if it be possible, let this cup pass from me; nevertheless, not as I will, but as you will." ⁴⁰And Jesus came to the disciples and found them sleeping, and said to Peter, "So, could you not watch with me one hour? ⁴¹Watch and pray that you may not enter into temptation; the spirit indeed is willing, but the flesh is weak." ⁴²Again, for the second time, Jesus went away and prayed, "[God] my Father [and Mother*], if this cannot pass unless I drink it, your will be done." ⁴³And again Jesus came and found them sleeping, for their eyes were heavy. ⁴⁴So, leaving them again, Jesus went away and prayed for the third time, saying the same words. ⁴⁵Then coming to the disciples Jesus said to them, "Are you still sleeping and taking your rest? Behold, the hour is at hand, and the Human One° is betrayed into the hands of sinners. ⁴⁶Rise, let us be going; see, my betrayer is at hand."

⁴⁷While Jesus was still speaking, Judas came, one of the twelve, and with him a great crowd with swords and clubs, from the chief priests and the elders of the people. ⁴⁸Now the betrayer had given them a sign, saying, "The one I shall kiss is the person; seize him." ⁴⁹And Judas came up to Jesus at once and said, "Hail, Teacher!" And Judas kissed Jesus. ⁵⁰Jesus said to Judas, "Friend, why are you here?" Then they came up and laid hands on Jesus and seized him. ⁵¹And behold, one of those who were with Jesus stretched out his hand and drew his sword and struck the slave of the high priest, and cut off his ear. ⁵²Then Jesus said to the disciple, "Put your sword back into its place; for all who take the sword will perish by the sword. ⁵³Do you think that I cannot appeal to [God] my Father [and Mother*], who will at once send me more than twelve legions of angels? ⁵⁴But how then should the scriptures be fulfilled, that it must be so?" ⁵⁵At that hour Jesus said to the crowds, "Have you come out as against a robber, with swords and clubs to capture me? Day after day I sat in the temple teaching, and you did not seize me. ⁵⁶But all this has taken place, that the scriptures of the prophets might be fulfilled." Then all the disciples forsook Jesus and fled.

---

*Addition to the text. RSV vs. 39, 42 *My Father;* v. 53 *my Father.* See "Metaphor" and "God the Father and Mother" in the Appendix.
°RSV *Son of man.* See Appendix.

⁵⁷Then those who had seized Jesus led him to Caiaphas the high priest, where the scribes and the elders had gathered. ⁵⁸But Peter followed Jesus at a distance, as far as the courtyard of the high priest, and going inside Peter sat with the guards to see the end. ⁵⁹Now the chief priests and the whole council sought false testimony against Jesus that they might put Jesus to death, ⁶⁰but they found none, though many false witnesses came forward. At last two came forward ⁶¹and said, "This one said, 'I am able to destroy the temple of God, and to build it in three days.' " ⁶²And the high priest stood up and said, "Have you no answer to make? What is it that these people testify against you?" ⁶³But Jesus was silent. And the high priest said to Jesus, "I adjure you by the living God, tell us if you are the Christ, the Child° of God." ⁶⁴Jesus replied, "You have said so. But I tell you, hereafter you will see the Human One° seated at the right hand of Power, and coming on the clouds of heaven." ⁶⁵Then the high priest tore his robes, and said, "This one has uttered blasphemy. Why do we still need witnesses? You have now heard the blasphemy. ⁶⁶What is your judgment?" They answered, "This one deserves death." ⁶⁷Then they spat in Jesus' face, and struck him; and some slapped Jesus, ⁶⁸saying, "Prophesy to us, you Christ! Who is it that struck you?"

⁶⁹Now Peter was sitting outside in the courtyard. And a maid came up and said, "You also were with Jesus the Galilean." ⁷⁰But Peter denied it before them all, saying, "I do not know what you mean." ⁷¹And when Peter went out to the porch, another maid saw him, and she said to the bystanders, "This one was with Jesus of Nazareth." ⁷²And again Peter denied it with an oath, "I do not know the man." ⁷³After a little while the bystanders came up and said to Peter, "Certainly you are also one of them, for your accent betrays you." ⁷⁴Then Peter began to invoke a curse on himself and to swear, "I do not know the man." And immediately the cock crowed. ⁷⁵And Peter remembered the saying of Jesus, "Before the cock crows, you will deny me three times." And Peter went out and wept bitterly.

²⁷:¹When morning came, all the chief priests and the elders of the people took counsel against Jesus to put him to death; ²and they bound and led Jesus away and delivered him to Pilate the governor.

³When Judas, the betrayer, saw that Jesus was condemned, Judas repented and brought back the thirty pieces of silver to the chief priests and the elders, ⁴saying, "I have sinned in betraying innocent blood." They said, "What is that to us? See to it yourself." ⁵And throwing down the pieces of silver in the temple, Judas departed, and went and hanged himself. ⁶But the chief priests, taking the pieces of silver, said, "It is not lawful to put

---

°RSV *Son.* See Appendix.
°RSV *Son of man.* See Appendix.

them into the treasury, since they are blood money." ⁷So they took counsel, and bought with them the potter's field, to bury strangers in. ⁸Therefore that field has been called the Field of Blood to this day. ⁹Then was fulfilled what had been spoken by the prophet Jeremiah, saying, "And they took the thirty pieces of silver, the price of the one on whom a price had been set by some of the children of Israel, ¹⁰and they gave them for the potter's field, as the Sovereign One□ directed me."

¹¹Now Jesus stood before the governor; and the governor asked, "Are you the Ruler□ of the Jews?" Jesus said, "You have said so." ¹²But when accused by the chief priests and elders, Jesus made no answer. ¹³Then Pilate said to Jesus, "Do you not hear how many things they testify against you?" ¹⁴But Jesus gave Pilate no answer, not even to a single charge; so that the governor wondered greatly.

¹⁵Now at the feast the governor was accustomed to release for the crowd any one prisoner whom they wanted. ¹⁶And they had then a notorious prisoner, called Barabbas. ¹⁷So when they had gathered, Pilate said to them, "Whom do you want me to release for you, Barabbas or Jesus who is called Christ?" ¹⁸For Pilate knew that it was out of envy that they had delivered Jesus up. ¹⁹Besides, while Pilate was sitting on the judgment seat, his wife sent word, "Have nothing to do with that righteous person, for I have suffered much over him today in a dream." ²⁰Now the chief priests and the elders persuaded the people to ask for Barabbas and destroy Jesus. ²¹The governor again said to them, "Which of the two do you want me to release for you?" And they said, "Barabbas." ²²Pilate said to them, "Then what shall I do with Jesus who is called Christ?" They all said, "Let Jesus be crucified." ²³And Pilate said, "Why, what evil has Jesus done?" But they shouted all the more, "Let Jesus be crucified."

²⁴So when Pilate saw that nothing was being gained, but rather that a riot was beginning, Pilate took water and washed his hands before the crowd, saying, "I am innocent of this person's blood; see to it yourselves." ²⁵And all the people answered, "Jesus' blood be on us and on our children!" ²⁶Then Pilate released for them Barabbas, and having scourged Jesus, delivered him to be crucified.

²⁷Then the soldiers of the governor took Jesus into the praetorium, and they gathered the whole battalion before him. ²⁸And they stripped Jesus and put a scarlet robe upon him, ²⁹and plaiting a crown of thorns they put it on Jesus' head, and put a reed in his right hand. And kneeling down, they mocked Jesus, saying, "Hail, Ruler□ of the Jews!" ³⁰And they spat upon Jesus, and took the reed and struck him on the head. ³¹And when they had mocked Jesus, they stripped him of the robe, and put Jesus' own clothes on him, and led Jesus away to be crucified.

□RSV *Lord*. See Appendix.
□RSV *King*. See Appendix.

^{32}As they went out, they came upon a Cyrenian, Simon by name, whom they compelled to carry Jesus' cross. ^{33}And when they came to a place called Golgotha (which means the place of a skull), ^{34}they offered Jesus wine to drink, mingled with gall; but after tasting it, Jesus would not drink it. ^{35}And when they had crucified Jesus, they divided his garments among them by casting lots; ^{36}then they sat down and kept watch over Jesus there. ^{37}And over Jesus' head they put the charge against him, which read, "This is Jesus the Ruler□ of the Jews." ^{38}Then two robbers were crucified with Jesus, one on the right and one on the left. ^{39}And those who passed by derided Jesus, wagging their heads ^{40}and saying, "You who would destroy the temple and build it in three days, save yourself! If you are the Child◇ of God, come down from the cross." ^{41}So also the chief priests, with the scribes and elders, mocked Jesus, saying, ^{42}"This one saved others, but cannot save himself. Jesus is the Ruler□ of Israel; let Jesus come down now from the cross, and we will believe in him. ^{43}Jesus trusts in God; let God deliver Jesus now, if God desires to; for Jesus said, 'I am the Child◇ of God.' " ^{44}And the robbers who were crucified also reviled him in the same way.

^{45}Now from the sixth hour there was darkness over all the land until the ninth hour. ^{46}And about the ninth hour Jesus cried with a loud voice, "Eli, Eli, lama sabach-thani?" that is, "My God, my God, why have you forsaken me?" ^{47}And some of the bystanders hearing it said, "This one is calling Elijah." ^{48}And one of them at once ran and took a sponge, filled it with vinegar, and put it on a reed, and gave it to Jesus to drink. ^{49}But the others said, "Wait, let us see whether Elijah will come to save him." ^{50}And Jesus cried again with a loud voice and yielded up his spirit.

^{51}And behold, the curtain of the temple was torn in two, from top to bottom; and the earth shook, and the rocks were split; ^{52}the tombs also were opened, and many bodies of the saints who had fallen asleep were raised, ^{53}and coming out of the tombs after the resurrection they went into the holy city and appeared to many. ^{54}When the centurion and those who were with him, keeping watch over Jesus, saw the earthquake and what took place, they were filled with awe, and said, "Truly this was the Child◇ of God!"

^{55}There were also many women there, looking on from afar, who had followed Jesus from Galilee, ministering to him; ^{56}among whom were Mary Magdalene, and Mary the mother of James and Joseph, and the mother of James and John, who were also sons of Zebedee.

^{57}When it was evening, there came a rich man from Arimathea, named Joseph, who also was a disciple of Jesus. ^{58}Joseph went to Pilate and asked

---

□RSV *King.* See Appendix.
◇RSV *Son.* See Appendix.

for the body of Jesus. Then Pilate ordered it to be given to him. [59]And Joseph took the body, and wrapped it in a clean linen shroud, [60]and laid it in his own new tomb, which had been hewn in the rock; and Joseph rolled a great stone to the door of the tomb, and departed. [61]Mary Magdalene and the other Mary were there, sitting opposite the sepulchre.

[62]Next day, that is, after the day of Preparation, the chief priests and the Pharisees gathered before Pilate [63]and said, "Sir, we remember how that impostor, while still alive, said, 'After three days I will rise again.' [64]Therefore order the sepulchre to be made secure until the third day, lest the disciples go and steal Jesus away, and tell the people, 'He has risen from the dead,' and the last fraud will be worse than the first." [65]Pilate said to them, "You have a guard of soldiers; go, make it as secure as you can." [66]So they went and made the sepulchre secure by sealing the stone and setting a guard.

MAUNDY THURSDAY

Lesson 1 ~ Exodus 12:1-14

God instructs Israel on keeping the first Passover.

¹GOD said to Moses and Aaron in the land of Egypt, ²"This month shall be for you the beginning of months; it shall be the first month of the year for you. ³Tell all the congregation of Israel that on the tenth day of this month they shall take every one a lamb according to their families' houses, a lamb for a household; ⁴and if the household is too small for a lamb, two households shall take according to the number of persons; according to what each can eat you shall make your count for the lamb. ⁵Your lamb shall be without blemish, a male a year old; you shall take it from the sheep or from the goats; ⁶and you shall keep it until the fourteenth day of this month, when the whole assembly of the congregation of Israel shall kill their lambs in the evening. ⁷Then they shall take some of the blood, and put it on the two doorposts and the lintel of the houses in which they eat them. ⁸They shall eat the flesh that night, roasted; with unleavened bread and bitter herbs they shall eat it. ⁹Do not eat any of it raw or boiled with water, but roasted, its head with its legs and its inner parts. ¹⁰And you shall let none of it remain until the morning, anything that remains until the morning you shall burn. ¹¹In this manner you shall eat it: your loins girded, your sandals on your feet, and your staff in your hand; and you shall eat it in haste. It is the passover of GOD. ¹²For I will pass through the land of Egypt that night, and I will smite all the first-born in the land of Egypt, both human and animal; and on all the gods of Egypt I will execute judgments: I am the SOVEREIGN ONE. ¹³The blood shall be a sign for you, upon the houses where you are; and when I see the blood, I will pass over you, and no plague shall fall upon you to destroy you, when I smite the land of Egypt.

¹⁴"This day shall be for you a memorial day, and you shall keep it as a feast to GOD; throughout your generations you shall observe it as an ordinance for ever."

Lesson 2 ~ 1 Corinthians 11:17-32

Paul writes to the Corinthians concerning the Last Supper.

¹⁷But in the following instructions I do not commend you, because when you come together it is not for the better but for the worse. ¹⁸For, in the first place, when you assemble as a church, I hear that there are divisions among you; and I partly believe it, ¹⁹for there must be factions among you in order that those who are genuine among you may be

recognized. [20]When you meet together, it is not the Sovereign's□ supper that you eat. [21]For in eating, each one goes ahead with their own meal, and one is hungry and another is drunk. [22]What! Do you not have houses to eat and drink in? Or do you despise the church of God and humiliate those who have nothing? What shall I say to you? Shall I commend you in this? No, I will not.

[23]For I received from the Sovereign□ what I also delivered to you, that the Sovereign□ Jesus on the night of the betrayal took bread, [24]and after giving thanks, broke it, and said, "This is my body which is for you. Do this in remembrance of me." [25]In the same way also the cup, after supper, saying, "This cup is the new covenant in my blood. Do this, as often as you drink it, in remembrance of me." [26]For as often as you eat this bread and drink the cup, you proclaim the Sovereign's□ death until Christ comes.

[27]Whoever, therefore, eats the bread or drinks the cup of the Sovereign□ in an unworthy manner will be guilty of profaning the body and blood of Christ. [28]Let all examine themselves, and so eat of the bread and drink of the cup. [29]For all who eat and drink without discerning the body eat and drink judgment upon themselves. [30]That is why many of you are weak and ill, and some have died. [31]But if we judged ourselves truly, we should not be judged. [32]But when we are judged by the Sovereign,□ we are chastened so that we may not be condemned along with the world.

Gospel ~ John 13:1-17, 34

Jesus washes the disciples' feet.

[1]Now before the feast of the Passover, when Jesus knew that the hour had come to depart out of this world to [God] the Father [and Mother*], having loved his own who were in the world, Jesus loved them to the end. [2]And during supper, when the devil had already put it into the heart of Judas Iscariot, Simon's son, to betray Jesus, [3]Jesus, knowing that God had given all things into Jesus' own hands, and that he had come from God and was going to God, [4]rose from supper, laid aside his garments, and girded himself with a towel. [5]Then Jesus poured water into a basin, and began to wash the disciples' feet, and to wipe them with the towel with which he was girded. [6]Jesus came to Simon Peter; and Peter said to him, "My

---

□RSV v. 20 *Lord's*; v. 23 *Lord*; v. 26 *Lord's*; v. 27 *Lord*; v. 32 *Lord*. See Appendix.
*Addition to the text. See "Metaphor" and "God the Father and Mother" in the Appendix.

Sovereign,□ do you wash my feet?" ⁷Jesus answered, "What I am doing you do not know now, but afterward you will understand." ⁸Peter said to Jesus, "You shall never wash my feet." Jesus answered, "If I do not wash you, you have no part in me." ⁹Simon Peter said to Jesus, "My Sovereign,□ not my feet only but also my hands and my head!" ¹⁰Jesus said to Peter, "One who has bathed does not need to wash, except for the feet, but is clean all over; and you are clean, but not every one of you." ¹¹For Jesus knew who was to betray him; that was why he said, "You are not all clean."

¹²Having washed their feet, and put on his garments, and returned to the table, Jesus said to them, "Do you know what I have done to you? ¹³You call me Teacher and Sovereign;□ and you are right, for so I am. ¹⁴If I then, your Sovereign□ and Teacher, have washed your feet, you also ought to wash one another's feet. ¹⁵For I have given you an example, that you also should do as I have done to you. ¹⁶Truly, truly, I say to you, a servant is not greater than the one who is served; nor is one who is sent greater than the sender. ¹⁷If you know these things, blessed are you if you do them. . . .

³⁴"A new commandment I give to you, that you love one another; even as I have loved you, that you also love one another."

□RSV *Lord*. See Appendix.

GOOD FRIDAY

Lesson 1 ~ Isaiah 52:13–53:12

Isaiah writes of the Suffering Servant.

¹³Behold, my servant shall prosper,
  shall be exalted and lifted up,
  and shall be very high.
¹⁴As many were astonished at the one
  whose appearance was so marred, beyond human semblance,
  and whose form beyond that of human beings,
¹⁵so many nations will be startled;
  rulers[□] shall shut their mouths because of my servant;
 for that which has not been told them they shall see,
  and that which they have not heard they shall understand.
^{53:1}Who has believed what we have heard?
  And to whom has the arm of GOD been revealed?
 ²For the servant grew up before God like a young plant,
  and like a root out of dry ground,
 with no form or comeliness that we should admire,
  and no beauty that we should desire.
 ³The servant was despised and rejected by every one,
  was full of sorrows, and acquainted with grief,
 and as one from whom people hide their faces,
  was despised and not esteemed by us.
 ⁴Surely this one has borne our griefs
  and carried our sorrows;
 yet we esteemed the servant stricken,
  smitten by God, and afflicted.
 ⁵But this servant was wounded for our transgressions,
  was bruised for our iniquities,
 bore the chastisement that made us whole
  and the stripes by which we are healed.
 ⁶All we like sheep have gone astray;
  we have turned every one to our own way;
 and GOD has laid on this one
  the iniquity of us all.
 ⁷The servant was oppressed, and was afflicted,
  yet did not say a word;
 like a lamb that is led to the slaughter,
  and like a ewe that before her shearers is dumb,
  the servant did not say a word.

□RSV *kings.* See Appendix.

⁸By oppression and judgment the servant was taken away;
  and as for that one's generation, who considered
that the servant was cut off out of the land of the living,
  stricken for the transgression of my people?
⁹Although the servant had done no violence
  and spoken no deceit,
the servant was buried with the wicked,
  and with the rich in death.
¹⁰Yet it was the will of GOD to bruise
  and put to grief this one;
who, after choosing to become an offering for sin,
  shall see offspring, and enjoy long life;
the will of GOD shall prosper in the servant's hand;
¹¹ my servant shall see the fruit of the soul's travail and be satisfied;
  by knowledge shall the righteous one, my servant,
    make many to be accounted righteous,
    and shall bear their iniquities.
¹²Therefore I will divide for this one a portion with the great,
  and my servant shall divide the spoil with the strong;
because my servant poured out self unto death,
  and was numbered with the transgressors;
yet bore the sin of many,
  and made intercession for the transgressors.

Lesson 2 ~ Hebrews 4:14-16; 5:7-9

Jesus the high priest learns obedience through suffering.

¹⁴Since then we have a great high priest who has passed through the heavens, Jesus, the Child° of God, let us hold fast our confession. ¹⁵For we have not a high priest who is unable to sympathize with our weaknesses, but one who in every respect has been tempted as we are, yet without sin. ¹⁶Let us then with confidence draw near to the throne of grace, that we may receive mercy and find grace to help in time of need. . . .

5:7While still in the flesh, Jesus offered up prayers and supplications, with loud cries and tears, to God who was able to save him from death, and was heard for his godly fear. ⁸Although the Child° of God, Jesus learned obedience through suffering; ⁹and being made perfect, became the source of eternal salvation to all who obey.

°RSV *Son*. See Appendix.

Lesson 2 (alternate) ~ Hebrews 10:1-25

Jesus the high priest offered a single sacrifice for our sins.

¹For since the law has but a shadow of the good things to come instead of the true form of these realities, it can never, by the same sacrifices which are continually offered year after year, make perfect those who draw near. ²Otherwise, would they not have ceased to be offered? If the worshipers had once been cleansed, they would no longer have any consciousness of sin. ³But in these sacrifices there is a reminder of sin year after year. ⁴For it is impossible that the blood of bulls and goats should take away sins.

⁵Consequently, Christ, having come into the world, said,

"Sacrifices and offerings you have not desired,

but a body you have prepared for me;

⁶in burnt offerings and sin offerings you have taken no pleasure.

⁷Then I said, 'Lo, I have come to do your will, O God,'

as it is written of me in the roll of the book."

⁸When Christ said above, "You have neither desired nor taken pleasure in sacrifices and offerings and burnt offerings and sin offerings" (these are offered according to the law), ⁹then Christ added, "Lo, I have come to do your will." Christ abolishes the first in order to establish the second. ¹⁰And by that will we have been sanctified through the offering of the body of Jesus Christ once for all.

¹¹And every priest stands daily at services, offering repeatedly the same sacrifices, which can never take away sins. ¹²But this one, having offered for all time a single sacrifice for sins, sat down at the right hand of God, ¹³then to wait until all enemies should be made a stool for Christ's feet. ¹⁴For by a single offering Christ has perfected for all time those who are sanctified. ¹⁵And the Holy Spirit also bears witness to us; for after saying,

¹⁶"This is the covenant that I will make with them

after those days, says the Sovereign:▯

I will put my laws on their hearts, and write them on their minds,"

¹⁷ then it is added,

"I will remember their sins and their misdeeds no more."

¹⁸Where there is forgiveness of these, there is no longer any offering for sin.

¹⁹Therefore, brothers and sisters, since we have confidence to enter the sanctuary by the blood of Jesus, ²⁰by the new and living way which Jesus opened for us through the curtain, that is, through Jesus' flesh, ²¹and since we have a great priest over the house of God, ²²let us draw near with a true heart in full assurance of faith, with our hearts sprinkled clean from an evil

---

▯RSV *Lord.* See Appendix.

conscience and our bodies washed with pure water. ²³Let us hold fast the confession of our hope without wavering, for the one who promised is faithful; ²⁴and let us consider how to stir up one another to love and good works, ²⁵not neglecting to meet together, as is the habit of some, but encouraging one another, and all the more as you see the Day drawing near.

Gospel ~ John 18:1–19:42

John recounts the arrest and death of Jesus.

¹After praying for the disciples, Jesus went forth with them across the Kidron valley, where there was a garden, which they entered. ²Now Judas, who betrayed Jesus, also knew the place; for Jesus often met there with the disciples. ³So Judas, procuring a band of soldiers and some officers from the chief priests and the Pharisees, went there with lanterns and torches and weapons. ⁴Then Jesus, knowing all that was to befall him, came forward and said to them, "Whom do you seek?" ⁵They answered, "Jesus of Nazareth." Jesus said to them, "I AM." Judas, the betrayer, was standing with them. ⁶When Jesus said to them, "I AM," they drew back and fell to the ground. ⁷Again Jesus asked them, "Whom do you seek?" And they said, "Jesus of Nazareth." ⁸Jesus answered, "I told you that I AM; so, if you seek me, let these others go." ⁹This was to fulfil the word which Jesus had spoken, "Of those whom you gave me I lost not one." ¹⁰Then Simon Peter, having a sword, drew it and struck the high priest's slave and cut off his right ear. The slave's name was Malchus. ¹¹Jesus said to Peter, "Put your sword into its sheath; shall I not drink the cup which [*God*] the Father [*and Mother**] has given me?"

¹²So the band of soldiers and their captain and the officers of the Jews seized and bound Jesus. ¹³First they led him to Annas, who was the father-in-law of Caiaphas, the high priest that year. ¹⁴It was Caiaphas who had given counsel to the Jews that it was expedient that one person should die for the people.

¹⁵Simon Peter followed Jesus, and so did another disciple, who was known to the high priest, and who entered the court of the high priest along with Jesus, ¹⁶while Peter stood outside at the door. So the other disciple, who was known to the high priest, went out and spoke to the maid who kept the door, and brought Peter in. ¹⁷The maid who kept the door said to Peter, "Are you not also one of this person's disciples?" Peter said, "I am not." ¹⁸Now the servants and officers had made a charcoal fire, because it was

---

*Addition to the text. See "Metaphor" and "God the Father and Mother" in the Appendix.

cold, and they were standing and warming themselves; Peter also was with them, standing and warming himself.

¹⁹The high priest then questioned Jesus about his disciples and teaching. ²⁰Jesus answered the high priest, "I have spoken openly to the world; I have always taught in synagogues and in the temple, where all Jews come together; I have said nothing secretly. ²¹Why do you ask me? Ask those who have heard me, what I said to them; they know what I said." ²²When Jesus had said this, one of the officers standing by struck Jesus with his hand, saying, "Is that how you answer the high priest?" ²³Jesus answered the officer, "If I have spoken wrongly, bear witness to the wrong; but if I have spoken rightly, why do you strike me?" ²⁴Annas then sent Jesus bound to Caiaphas the high priest.

²⁵Now Simon Peter was standing and warming himself. They said to Peter, "Are not you also one of the disciples?" He denied it and said, "I am not." ²⁶One of the servants of the high priest, a relative of the slave whose ear Peter had cut off, asked, "Did I not see you in the garden with this person?" ²⁷Peter again denied it; and at once the cock crowed.

²⁸Then they led Jesus from the house of Caiaphas to the praetorium. It was early. They themselves did not enter the praetorium, so that they might not be defiled, but might eat the passover. ²⁹So Pilate went out to them and said, "What accusation do you bring against this person?" ³⁰They answered Pilate, "If this one were not an evildoer, we would not have handed him over." ³¹Pilate said to them, "Take this person yourselves and make judgment by your own law." The Jews said to Pilate, "It is not lawful for us to put any one to death." ³²This was to fulfil the word which Jesus had spoken to show by what death he was to die.

³³Pilate entered the praetorium again and called Jesus, and said, "Are you the Ruler⊡ of the Jews?" ³⁴ Jesus answered, "Do you say this of your own accord, or did others say it to you about me?" ³⁵Pilate answered, "Am I a Jew? Your own nation and the chief priests have handed you over to me; what have you done?" ³⁶Jesus answered, "My realm* is not of this world; if my realm* were of this world, my servants would fight, that I might not be handed over to the Jews; but my realm* is not from the world." ³⁷Pilate said to Jesus, "So you are a ruler?"⊡ Jesus answered, "You say that I am a ruler.⊡ For this I was born, and for this I have come into the world, to bear witness to the truth. Every one who is of the truth hears my voice." ³⁸Pilate said to him, "What is truth?"

And having said this, Pilate went out to the Jews again, and told them, "I find no crime in this person. ³⁹But you have a custom that I should

---

⊡RSV v. 33 *King*; v. 37 *king*. See Appendix.
*RSV *kingship*.

release someone for you at the Passover; will you have me release for you the Ruler□ of the Jews?" ⁴⁰They cried out again, "Not Jesus, but Barabbas!" Now Barabbas was a robber.

19:1Then Pilate had Jesus scourged. ²And the soldiers plaited a crown of thorns, and put it on Jesus' head, and arrayed Jesus in a purple robe; ³they came up, saying, "Hail, Ruler□ of the Jews!" and struck Jesus with their hands. ⁴Pilate went out again, and said to them, "See, I am bringing this person out to you, that you may know that I find no crime in him." ⁵So Jesus came out, wearing the crown of thorns and the purple robe. Pilate said to them, "Here is the one!" ⁶When the chief priests and the officers saw Jesus, they cried out, "Crucify, crucify!" Pilate said to them, "Take this one yourselves and crucify him, for I find no crime in Jesus." ⁷The Jews answered Pilate, "We have a law, and by that law Jesus ought to die, having made himself the Child◇ of God." ⁸Hearing these words, Pilate was the more afraid. ⁹Pilate entered the praetorium again and said to Jesus, "Where are you from?" But Jesus gave no answer. ¹⁰Pilate therefore said to Jesus, "You will not speak to me? Do you not know that I have power to release you, and power to crucify you?" ¹¹Jesus answered Pilate, "You would have no power over me unless it had been given you from above; therefore the one who delivered me to you has the greater sin."

¹²Upon this Pilate sought to release Jesus, but the Jews cried out, "If you release this person, you are not Caesar's friend; every one who claims to be a ruler□ opposes Caesar." ¹³Hearing these words, Pilate brought Jesus out and sat down on the judgment seat at a place called The Pavement, and in Hebrew, Gabbatha. ¹⁴Now it was the day of Preparation of the Passover; it was about the sixth hour. Pilate said to the Jews, "Behold your Ruler!"□ ¹⁵They cried out, "Get on with it, get on with it, crucify Jesus!" Pilate said to them, "Shall I crucify your Ruler?"□ The chief priests answered, "We have no ruler□ but Caesar." ¹⁶Then Pilate handed Jesus over to them to be crucified.

¹⁷So they took Jesus, who went out bearing his own cross, to the place called the place of a skull, which is called in Hebrew Golgotha. ¹⁸There they crucified Jesus, along with two others, one on either side, and Jesus between them. ¹⁹Pilate also wrote a title and put it on the cross; it read, "Jesus of Nazareth, the Ruler□ of the Jews." ²⁰Many of the Jews read this title, for the place where Jesus was crucified was near the city; and it was written in Hebrew, in Latin, and in Greek. ²¹The chief priests of the Jews then said to Pilate, "Do not write, 'The Ruler□ of the Jews,' but, 'This one

---

□RSV v. 39 and 19:3 *King;* v. 12 *king;* v. 14 *King;* v. 15 *King, king;* vs. 19, 21 *King.* See Appendix.
◇RSV *Son.* See Appendix.

said, I am Ruler⊡ of the Jews.' " ²²Pilate answered, "What I have written I have written."

²³When the soldiers had crucified Jesus they took his garments and made four parts, one for each soldier; also Jesus' tunic. But the tunic was without seam, woven from top to bottom; ²⁴so they said to one another, "Let us not tear it, but cast lots for it to see whose it shall be." This was to fulfil the scripture,

> "They parted my garments among them,
> and for my clothing they cast lots."

²⁵So the soldiers did this. But standing by the cross of Jesus were his mother, and his mother's sister, Mary the wife of Clopas, and Mary Magdalene. ²⁶When Jesus saw his mother, and the disciple whom he loved standing near, Jesus said to his mother, "Woman, behold, your child!" ²⁷Then Jesus said to the disciple, "Behold, your mother!" And from that hour the disciple took her to his own home.

²⁸After this Jesus, knowing that all was now finished, said (to fulfil the scripture), "I thirst." ²⁹A bowl full of vinegar stood there; so they put a sponge full of the vinegar on hyssop and held it to Jesus' mouth. ³⁰After receiving the vinegar, Jesus said, "It is finished"; and Jesus bowed his head and gave up the spirit.

³¹Since it was the day of Preparation, in order to prevent the bodies from remaining on the cross on the sabbath (for that sabbath was a high day), the Jews asked Pilate that their legs might be broken, and that they might be taken away. ³²So the soldiers came and broke the legs of the first, and of the other who had been crucified with Jesus; ³³but when they came to Jesus and saw that he was already dead, they did not break his legs. ³⁴But one of the soldiers pierced Jesus' side with a spear, and at once there came out blood and water. ³⁵The one who saw it has borne witness—this testimony is true, and the witness knows that it is the truth—that you also may believe. ³⁶For these things took place that the scripture might be fulfilled, "Not a bone of that one shall be broken." ³⁷And again another scripture says, "They shall look on the one whom they have pierced."

³⁸After this Joseph of Arimathea, who was a disciple of Jesus, but secretly, for fear of the Jews, asked Pilate for permission to take away the body of Jesus, and Pilate granted it. So Joseph came and took away Jesus' body. ³⁹Nicodemus also, who had at first come to Jesus by night, came bringing a mixture of myrrh and aloes, about a hundred pounds' weight. ⁴⁰They took the body of Jesus, and bound it in linen cloths with the spices, as is the burial custom of the Jews. ⁴¹Now in the place where Jesus was crucified there was a garden, and in the garden a new tomb where no one had ever been laid. ⁴²So because of the Jewish day of Preparation, as the tomb was close at hand, they laid Jesus there.

⊡RSV *King*. See Appendix.

EASTER

Lesson 1 ~ Acts 10:34-48

Peter preaches about Jesus' life, death, and resurrection.

³⁴Peter proclaimed: "Truly I perceive that God shows no partiality, ³⁵but in every nation anyone who fears God and does what is right is acceptable to God. ³⁶You know the word which God sent to Israel, preaching good news of peace by Jesus Christ (Christ is Sovereign□ of all), ³⁷the word which was proclaimed throughout all Judea, beginning from Galilee after the baptism which John preached: ³⁸how God anointed Jesus of Nazareth with the Holy Spirit and with power; how Jesus went about doing good and healing all that were oppressed by the devil, for God was with Jesus. ³⁹And we are witnesses to all that Jesus did both in Judea and in Jerusalem. They put Jesus to death by hanging him on a tree; ⁴⁰but God raised Jesus on the third day and made Jesus manifest; ⁴¹not to all the people but to us who were chosen by God as witnesses, who ate and drank with Jesus after Jesus' resurrection from the dead. ⁴²And Jesus commanded us to preach to the people, and to testify that this one is the one ordained by God to be judge of the living and the dead. ⁴³To this one all the prophets bear witness that every one who believes in Jesus Christ receives forgiveness of sins through this name."

⁴⁴While Peter was still saying this, the Holy Spirit fell on all who heard the word. ⁴⁵And the believers from among the Jews who came with Peter were amazed, because the gift of the Holy Spirit had been poured out even on the Gentiles. ⁴⁶For they heard them speaking in tongues and extolling God. Then Peter declared, ⁴⁷"Can any one forbid water for baptizing these people who have received the Holy Spirit just as we have?" ⁴⁸And Peter commanded them to be baptized in the name of Jesus Christ. Then they asked Peter to remain for some days.

Lesson 1 (alternate) ~ Exodus 14:10-14, 21-25; 15:20-21

The Hebrew slaves escape their pursuers.

¹⁰When Pharaoh drew near, the people of Israel lifted up their eyes, and behold, the Egyptians were marching after them; and they were in great fear. And the people of Israel cried out to GOD; ¹¹and they said to Moses, "Is it because there are no graves in Egypt that you have taken us

---

□RSV *Lord.* See Appendix.

away to die in the wilderness? What have you done to us, in bringing us out of Egypt? ¹²Is not this what we said to you in Egypt, 'Let us alone and let us serve the Egyptians'? For it would have been better for us to serve the Egyptians than to die in the wilderness." ¹³And Moses said to the people, "Fear not, stand firm, and see the salvation which GOD will work for you today; for the Egyptians whom you see today, you shall never see again. ¹⁴GOD will fight for you, and you have only to be still." . . .

²¹Then Moses stretched out a hand over the sea; and GOD drove the sea back by a strong east wind all night, and made the sea dry land, and the waters were divided. ²²And the people of Israel went into the midst of the sea on dry ground, the waters being a wall to them on their right hand and on their left. ²³The Egyptians pursued, and went in after them into the midst of the sea, all Pharaoh's horses, chariots, and drivers. ²⁴And in the morning watch GOD in the pillar of fire and of cloud looked down upon the host of the Egyptians, and discomfited the host of the Egyptians, ²⁵clogging their chariot wheels so that they drove heavily; and the Egyptians said, "Let us flee from before Israel; for GOD fights for them against the Egyptians." . . .

¹⁵:²⁰Then Miriam, the prophet, the sister of Aaron, took a timbrel in her hand; and all the women went out after her with timbrels and dancing. ²¹And Miriam sang to them:

"Sing to the SOVEREIGN ONE, who has triumphed gloriously;
the horse and the rider God has thrown into the sea."

Lesson 2 ~ Colossians 3:1-11

The author writes about our new life in Christ.

¹If then you have been raised with Christ, seek the things that are above, where Christ is, seated at the right hand of God. ²Set your minds on things that are above, not on things that are on earth. ³For you have died, and your life is hid with Christ in God. ⁴When Christ who is our life appears, then you also will appear with Christ in glory.

⁵Put to death therefore what is earthly in you: fornication, impurity, passion, evil desire, and covetousness, which is idolatry. ⁶On account of these the wrath of God is coming. ⁷In these you once walked, when you lived in them. ⁸But now put them all away: anger, wrath, malice, slander, and foul talk from your mouth. ⁹Do not lie to one another, seeing that you have put off the old nature with its practices ¹⁰and have put on the new nature, which is being renewed in knowledge after the image of its creator. ¹¹Here there cannot be Greek and Jew, those who are under law and those who are not, barbarian, Scythian, slave, or free, but Christ is all, and in all.

Gospel ~ John 20:1-18

The risen Christ appears to Mary Magdalene.

¹Now on the first day of the week Mary Magdalene came to the tomb early, while it was still dark, and saw that the stone had been taken away from the tomb. ²So she ran, and went to Simon Peter and the other disciple, the one whom Jesus loved, and said to them, "They have taken the Sovereign□ out of the tomb, and we do not know where they have laid him." ³Peter then came out with the other disciple, and they went toward the tomb. ⁴They both ran, but the other disciple outran Peter, reached the tomb first, ⁵and stooping to look in, saw the linen cloths lying there, but did not go in. ⁶Then Simon Peter came, following after, and went into the tomb; Peter saw the linen cloths lying, ⁷and the napkin, which had been on Jesus' head, not lying with the linen cloths but rolled up in a place by itself. ⁸Then the other disciple, who reached the tomb first, also went in, and saw and believed; ⁹for as yet they did not know the scripture, that Jesus must rise from the dead. ¹⁰Then the disciples went back to their homes.

¹¹But Mary stood weeping outside the tomb, and as she wept she stooped to look into the tomb; ¹²and she saw two angels in white, sitting where the body of Jesus had lain, one at the head and one at the feet. ¹³They said to her, "Woman, why are you weeping?" She said to them, "Because they have taken away my Sovereign,□ and I do not know where they have laid him." ¹⁴Saying this, she turned round and saw Jesus standing, but she did not know that it was Jesus. ¹⁵Jesus said to her, "Woman, why are you weeping? Whom do you seek?" Supposing Jesus to be the gardener, she answered, "Sir, if you have carried Jesus away, tell me where you have laid him, and I will take him away." ¹⁶Jesus said to her, "Mary." She turned and responded in Hebrew, "Rabboni!" (which means Teacher). ¹⁷Jesus said to her, "Do not hold me, for I have not yet ascended to God; but go to my friends and say to them, I am ascending [*to God,*] to my Father [*and Mother**] and your Father [*and Mother**], to my God and your God." ¹⁸Mary Magdalene went and said to the disciples, "I have seen the Sovereign";□ and she told them that Jesus had said these things to her.

□RSV *Lord*. See Appendix.
*Addition to the text. See "Metaphor" and "God the Father and Mother" in the Appendix.

Jesus appears to Mary Magdalene and the other Mary.

[1]Now after the sabbath, toward the dawn of the first day of the week, Mary Magdalene and the other Mary went to see the sepulchre. [2]And behold, there was a great earthquake; for an angel of God descended from heaven and came and rolled back the stone, and sat upon it. [3]The angel's appearance was like lightning, and its raiment white as snow. [4]And for fear of the angel the guards trembled and became like dead people. [5]But the angel said to the women, "Do not be afraid; for I know that you seek Jesus who was crucified. [6]Jesus is not here, but has risen, as he said. Come, see the place where Jesus lay. [7]Then go quickly and tell the disciples that Jesus has risen from the dead, and behold, even now is going before you to Galilee. There you will see Jesus. Lo, I have told you." [8]So they departed quickly from the tomb with fear and great joy, and ran to tell the disciples. [9]And behold, Jesus met them and said, "Hail!" And they came up and took hold of Jesus' feet and worshiped Jesus. [10]Then Jesus said to them, "Do not be afraid; go and tell my followers to go to Galilee, and there they will see me."

EASTER 2

Lesson 1 ～ Acts 2:14a, 22-32

Peter preaches his sermon at Pentecost.

[14]Peter, standing with the eleven, addressed them, . . .
[22]"People of Israel, hear these words: Jesus of Nazareth, attested to you by God with mighty works and wonders and signs which God did through him in your midst, as you yourselves know—[23]this Jesus, delivered up according to the definite plan and foreknowledge of God, you crucified and killed by the hands of lawless people. [24]But God raised Jesus up, having loosed the pangs of death, because it was not possible for him to be held by it. [25]For David has already said,

'I saw the Sovereign□ always before me,
  who is at my right hand that I may not be shaken;
[26]therefore my heart was glad, and my tongue rejoiced;
  moreover my flesh will dwell in hope.
[27]For you will not abandon my soul to Hades,
  nor let your Holy One see corruption.
[28]You have made known to me the ways of life;
  you will make me full of gladness with your presence.'

[29]"Brothers and sisters, I may say to you confidently that David both died and was buried, and his tomb is with us to this day. [30]Being therefore a prophet, and knowing that God had sworn to set one of David's own descendants upon the throne, [31]David foresaw and spoke of the resurrection of the Christ, who was not abandoned to Hades, and whose flesh did not see corruption. [32]This Jesus God raised up, and of that we all are witnesses."

Lesson 1 (alternate) ～ Genesis 8:6-16; 9:8-16

Noah sends forth a dove to see if the waters still cover the earth, and God makes a covenant with Noah.

[6]At the end of forty days Noah opened the window of the ark which had been made, [7]and sent forth a raven; and it went to and fro until the waters were dried up from the earth. [8]Then Noah sent forth a dove, to see if the waters had subsided from the face of the ground; [9]but the dove found no place to set its foot, and it returned to the ark, for the waters were still on

---

□RSV *Lord.* See Appendix.

the face of the whole earth. So Noah put forth his hand and took the dove and brought it into the ark. ¹⁰He waited another seven days and again sent forth the dove out of the ark; ¹¹and the dove came back in the evening, and lo, in its mouth a freshly plucked olive leaf; so Noah knew that the waters had subsided from the earth. ¹²Then he waited another seven days, and sent forth the dove; and it did not return to Noah any more.

¹³In the six hundred and first year, in the first month, the first day of the month, the waters were dried from off the earth; and Noah removed the covering of the ark, and looked, and behold, the face of the ground was dry. ¹⁴In the second month, on the twenty-seventh day of the month, the earth was dry. ¹⁵Then God said to Noah, ¹⁶"Go forth from the ark, you and your wife, and your sons and your daughters-in-law with you." . . .

⁹:⁸Then God said to Noah and to his family, ⁹"Behold, I establish my covenant with you and your descendants after you, ¹⁰and with every living creature that is with you, the birds, the cattle, and every beast of the earth with you, as many as came out of the ark. ¹¹I establish my covenant with you, that never again shall all flesh be cut off by the waters of a flood, and never again shall there be a flood to destroy the earth." ¹²And God said, "This is the sign of the covenant which I make between me and you and every living creature that is with you, for all future generations: ¹³I set my bow in the cloud, and it shall be a sign of the covenant between me and the earth. ¹⁴When I bring clouds over the earth and the bow is seen in the clouds, ¹⁵I will remember my covenant which is between me and you and every living creature of all flesh; and the waters shall never again become a flood to destroy all flesh. ¹⁶When the bow is in the clouds, I will look upon it and remember the everlasting covenant between God and every living creature of all flesh that is upon the earth."

Lesson 2 ~ 1 Peter 1:3-9

Peter speaks of God's great mercy in raising Christ from the dead.

³Blessed be God the Father [*and Mother**] of our Sovereign□ Jesus Christ! By God's great mercy we have been born anew to a living hope through the resurrection of Jesus Christ from the dead, ⁴and to an inheritance which is imperishable, undefiled, and unfading, kept in heaven for you, ⁵who by God's power are guarded through faith for a salvation ready to be revealed in the last time. ⁶In this you rejoice, though now for a little while you may have to suffer various trials, ⁷so that the genuineness of

---

*Addition to the text. RSV *the God and Father*. See "Metaphor" and "God the Father and Mother" in the Appendix.
□RSV *Lord*. See Appendix.

your faith, more precious than gold which though perishable is tested by fire, may redound to praise and glory and honor at the revelation of Jesus Christ, [8]whom not having seen, you love; and whom, though you do not now see, you yet believe in, and rejoice with unutterable and exalted joy. [9]As the outcome of your faith you obtain the salvation of your souls.

Gospel ~ John 20:19-31

The risen Christ appears to Thomas.

[19]On the evening of that day, the first day of the week, the doors being shut where the disciples were, for fear of the Jewish authorities, Jesus came and stood among them and said to them, "Peace be with you." [20]Having said this, Jesus showed them his hands and side. Then the disciples were glad when they saw the Sovereign.□ [21]Jesus said to them again, "Peace be with you. As [*God*] the [*Mother and**] Father has sent me, even so I send you." [22]Having said this, Jesus breathed on them, and said to them, "Receive the Holy Spirit. [23]If you forgive the sins of any, they are forgiven; if you retain the sins of any, they are retained."

[24]Now Thomas, one of the twelve, called the Twin, was not with them when Jesus came. [25]So the other disciples told him, "We have seen the Sovereign."□ But Thomas said to them, "Unless I see in Jesus' hands the print of the nails, and place my finger in the mark of the nails, and place my hand in Jesus' side, I will not believe."

[26]Eight days later, the disciples were again in the house, and Thomas was with them. The doors were shut, but Jesus came and stood among them, and said, "Peace be with you." [27]Then Jesus said to Thomas, "Put your finger here, and see my hands; and put out your hand, and place it in my side; do not be faithless, but believing." [28]Thomas answered, "My Sovereign□ and my God!" [29]Jesus said to Thomas, "Have you believed because you have seen me? Blessed are those who have not seen and yet believe."

[30]Now Jesus did many other signs in the presence of the disciples, which are not written in this book; [31]but these are written that you may believe that Jesus is the Christ, the Child° of God, and that believing you may have life in Christ's name.

□RSV *Lord*. See Appendix.
*Addition to the text. See "Metaphor" and "God the Father and Mother" in the Appendix.
°RSV *Son*. See Appendix.

EASTER 3

Lesson 1 ~ Acts 2:14a, 36-47

Peter's preaching leads to the conversion of many.

¹⁴Peter, standing with the eleven, addressed the Judeans, . . .

³⁶"Let all the house of Israel therefore know assuredly that God has made this Jesus whom you crucified both Sovereign□ and Christ."

³⁷Now when the Judeans heard this they were cut to the heart, and said to Peter and the rest of the apostles, "Brothers and sisters, what shall we do?" ³⁸And Peter said to them, "Repent, and be baptized every one of you in the name of Jesus Christ for the forgiveness of your sins; and you shall receive the gift of the Holy Spirit. ³⁹For the promise is to you and to your children and to all that are far off, every one whom the Sovereign□ our God calls." ⁴⁰And Peter testified with many other words and exhorted them, saying, "Save yourselves from this crooked generation." ⁴¹So those who received Peter's word were baptized, and there were added that day about three thousand souls. ⁴²And they devoted themselves to the apostles' teaching and community life, to the breaking of bread and the prayers.

⁴³And fear came upon every soul; and many wonders and signs were done through the apostles. ⁴⁴And all who believed were together and had all things in common; ⁴⁵and they sold their possessions and goods and distributed them to all, as any had need. ⁴⁶And day by day, attending the temple together and breaking bread in their homes, they partook of food with glad and generous hearts, ⁴⁷praising God and having favor with all the people. And the Sovereign□ added to their number day by day those who were being saved.

Lesson 1 (alternate) ~ Isaiah 43:1-12

God liberates exiled Israel.

¹But now thus says the SOVEREIGN ONE,
    who created you, O Jacob,
    who formed you, O Israel:
"Fear not, for I have redeemed you;
    I have called you by name, you are mine.
²When you pass through the waters I will be with you;
    and through the rivers, they shall not overwhelm you;
when you walk through fire you shall not be burned,
    and the flame shall not consume you.

□RSV *Lord.* See Appendix.

³For I am the Sovereign One your God,
  the Holy One of Israel, your Savior.
I give Egypt as your ransom,
  Ethiopia and Seba in exchange for you.
⁴Because you are precious in my eyes,
  and honored, and I love you,
I give human lives in return for you,
  peoples in exchange for your life.
⁵Fear not, for I am with you;
  I will bring your offspring from the east,
  and from the west I will gather you;
⁶I will say to the north, Give up,
  and to the south, Do not withhold;
bring my sons from afar
  and my daughters from the end of the earth,
⁷every one who is called by my name,
  whom I created for my glory,
  whom I formed and made."
⁸Bring forth the people who are blind, yet have eyes,
  who are deaf, yet have ears!
⁹Let all the nations gather together,
  and let the peoples assemble.
Who among them can declare this,
  and show us the former things?
Let them bring their witness to justify them,
  and let them hear and say, It is true.
¹⁰"You are my witnesses," says the Sovereign One,
  "and my servant whom I have chosen,
that you may know and believe me
  and understand that I am the One.
Before me no god was formed,
  nor shall there be any after me.
¹¹I, I am the Sovereign One,
  and besides me there is no savior.
¹²I declared and saved and proclaimed,
  when there was no strange god among you;
  and you are my witnesses," says the Sovereign One.

Lesson 2 ~ 1 Peter 1:17-23

The power of the risen Christ transforms our lives.

17And if you invoke as Father [*and Mother**] God who judges each one impartially according to each one's deeds, conduct yourselves with fear throughout the time of your exile. 18You know that you were ransomed from the futile ways inherited from your ancestors, not with perishable things such as silver or gold, 19but with the precious blood of Christ, like that of a lamb without blemish or spot. 20Christ was destined before the foundation of the world but was made manifest at the end of the times for your sake. 21You have confidence in God through Christ, whom God raised from the dead and glorified so that your faith and hope are in God.

22Having purified your souls by your obedience to the truth for a sincere love of each other, love one another earnestly from the heart. 23You have been born anew, not of perishable seed but of imperishable, through the living and abiding word of God.

Gospel ~ Luke 24:13-35

Jesus meets two disciples on the road to Emmaus.

13That very day two of the disciples were going to a village named Emmaus, about seven miles from Jerusalem, 14and talking with each other about all these things that had happened. 15While they were talking and discussing together, Jesus drew near and went with them. 16But their eyes were kept from recognizing him. 17And Jesus said to them, "What is this conversation which you are holding with each other as you walk?" And they stood still, looking sad. 18Then one of them, named Cleopas, answered, "Are you the only visitor to Jerusalem who does not know the things that have happened there in these days?" 19And Jesus said to them, "What things?" And they said, "Concerning Jesus of Nazareth, who was a prophet mighty in deed and word before God and all the people, 20and how our chief priests and rulers delivered this Jesus up to be condemned to death, and crucified him. 21But we had hoped that Jesus was the one to redeem Israel. Yes, and besides all this, it is now the third day since this happened. 22Moreover, some women of our company amazed us. They were at the tomb early in the morning 23and did not find Jesus' body; and they came back saying that they had even seen a vision of angels, who said that Jesus was alive. 24Some of those who were with us went to the tomb, and found it

---

*Addition to the text. See "Metaphor" and "God the Father and Mother" in the Appendix.

just as the women had said; but Jesus they did not see." ²⁵And Jesus said to them, "O foolish ones, and slow of heart to believe all that the prophets have spoken! ²⁶Was it not necessary that the Christ should suffer these things and be glorified?" ²⁷And beginning with Moses and all the prophets, Jesus interpreted to them in all the scriptures the things concerning himself.

²⁸So they drew near to the village to which they were going. Jesus appeared to be going further, ²⁹but they urged against it, saying, "Stay with us, for it is toward evening and the day is now far spent." So Jesus went in to stay with them. ³⁰When he was at table with them, Jesus took the bread and blessed, and broke it, and gave it to them. ³¹And their eyes were opened and they recognized Jesus, who then vanished out of their sight. ³²They said to each other, "Did not our hearts burn within us while Jesus talked to us on the road, and opened to us the scriptures?" ³³And they rose that same hour and returned to Jerusalem; and they found the eleven gathered together and those who were with them, ³⁴who said, "The Sovereign□ has risen indeed, and has appeared to Simon!" ³⁵Then they told what had happened on the road, and how Jesus was known to them in the breaking of the bread.

□RSV *Lord.* See Appendix.

EASTER 4

Lesson 1 ~ Acts 6:1-9; 7:2a, 51-56

Stephen, full of the Holy Spirit, preaches to the people.

[1]Now in these days when the disciples were increasing in number, the Hellenists murmured against the Hebrews because their widows were neglected in the daily distribution. [2]And the twelve summoned the body of the disciples and said, "It is not right that we should give up preaching the word of God to serve tables. [3]Therefore, sisters and brothers, pick out from among you seven people of good repute, full of the Spirit and of wisdom, whom we may appoint to this duty. [4]But we will devote ourselves to prayer and to the ministry of the word." [5]And what they said pleased the whole multitude, and they chose Stephen, who was full of faith and of the Holy Spirit, and Philip, and Prochorus, and Nicanor, and Timon, and Parmenas, and Nicolaus, a proselyte of Antioch. [6]These they set before the apostles, and they prayed and laid their hands upon them.

[7]And the word of God increased; and the number of the disciples multiplied greatly in Jerusalem, and a great many of the priests were obedient to the faith.

[8]And Stephen, full of grace and power, did great wonders and signs among the people. [9]Then some of those who belonged to the synagogue of the Libertines (as it was called), and of the Cyrenians, and of the Alexandrians, and of those from Cilicia and Asia, arose and disputed with Stephen. . . .

[7:2]And Stephen said: "Hear me, . . . [51]you stiff-necked people, insensitive in heart and ears, you always resist the Holy Spirit. As your ancestors did, so do you. [52]Which of the prophets did not your ancestors persecute? And they killed those who announced beforehand the coming of the Righteous One, whom you have now betrayed and murdered, [53]you who received the law as delivered by angels and did not keep it."

[54]Now when they heard these things they were enraged, and they ground their teeth against Stephen. [55]But Stephen, full of the Holy Spirit, gazed into heaven and saw the glory of God, and Jesus standing at the right hand of God; [56]and Stephen said, "Behold, I see the heavens opened, and the Human One° standing at the right hand of God."

°RSV *Son of man.* See Appendix.

Lesson 1 (alternate) ~ Nehemiah 9:6-15

Ezra recounts God's deliverance of Israel in the exodus.

⁶And Ezra said: "You are the Sovereign One, you alone; you have made heaven, the heaven of heavens, with all their host, the earth and all that is on it, the seas and all that is in them; and you preserve all of them; and the host of heaven worships you. ⁷You are the Sovereign One, the God who chose Abram and brought him forth out of Ur of the Chaldeans and gave him the name Abraham; ⁸and you found his heart faithful before you, and made with Abraham [*and Sarah**] the covenant to give to their descendants the land of the Canaanite, the Hittite, the Amorite, the Perizzite, the Jebusite, and the Girgashite; and you have fulfilled your promise, for you are righteous.

⁹"And you saw the affliction of our ancestors in Egypt and heard their cry at the Red Sea, ¹⁰and performed signs and wonders against Pharaoh and all his servants and all the people of his land, for you knew that they acted insolently against our ancestors; and you received a name, as it is to this day. ¹¹And you divided the sea before them, so that they went through the midst of the sea on dry land; and you cast their pursuers into the depths, as a stone into mighty waters. ¹²By a pillar of cloud you led them in the day, and by a pillar of fire in the night to light for them the way in which they should go. ¹³You came down upon Mount Sinai, and spoke with them from heaven and gave them right ordinances and true laws, good statutes and commandments, ¹⁴and you made known to them your holy sabbath and commanded them commandments and statutes and a law by Moses your servant. ¹⁵You gave them bread from heaven for their hunger and brought forth water for them from the rock for their thirst, and you told them to go in to possess the land which you had sworn to give them.

Lesson 2 ~ 1 Peter 2:19-25

Christ, who suffered and died for our sins, trusted in God, who judges justly.

¹⁹For you are approved if, mindful of God, you endure while suffering unjustly. ²⁰For what credit is it, if when you do wrong and are beaten for it you take it patiently? But if when you do right and suffer for it you take it patiently, you have God's approval. ²¹For to this you have been called, because Christ also suffered for you, leaving you an example, that you

---

*Addition to the text. See Appendix.

should follow in Christ's steps. [22]Christ committed no sin; and spoke without guile. [23]Though reviled, Christ did not revile in return; while suffering, Christ did not threaten, but trusted in God who judges justly, [24]bearing our sins in Christ's own body on the tree, that we might die to sin and live to righteousness. By Christ's wounds you have been healed. [25]For you were straying like sheep, but have now returned to the Shepherd and Guardian of your souls.

Gospel ∼ John 10:1-10

Jesus instructs the disciples in the parable of the good shepherd.

[1]"Truly, truly, I say to you, any one who does not enter the sheepfold by the door but climbs in by another way is a thief and a robber; [2]but the one who enters by the door is the shepherd of the sheep. [3]To this one the gatekeeper opens; the sheep hear the voice, and the shepherd calls them by name and leads them out. [4]After bringing out all of the shepherd's very own sheep, the shepherd goes before them, and the sheep follow, for they know the shepherd's voice. [5]A stranger they will not follow, but they will flee away, for they do not know the voice of strangers." [6]This figure Jesus used with the disciples, but they did not understand what he was saying to them.

[7]So Jesus said again, "Truly, truly, I say to you, I am the door of the sheep. [8]All who came before me are thieves and robbers; but the sheep did not heed them. [9]I am the door; whoever enters by me will be saved, and will go in and out and find pasture. [10]The thief comes only to steal and kill and destroy; I came that they may have life, and have it abundantly."

EASTER 5

Paul preaches in Thessalonica.

¹Now when Paul and Silas had passed through Amphipolis and Apollonia, they came to Thessalonica, where there was a synagogue of the Jews. ²And Paul went in, as was his custom, and for three weeks argued with them from the scriptures, ³explaining and proving that it was necessary for the Christ to suffer and to rise from the dead, and saying, "This Jesus, whom I proclaim to you, is the Christ." ⁴And some of them were persuaded, and joined Paul and Silas; as did a great many of the devout Greeks and not a few of the leading women. ⁵But the Jews were jealous, and taking a gang from the market place, they gathered a crowd, set the city in an uproar, and attacked the house of Jason, seeking to bring Paul and Silas out to the people. ⁶And when the Jews could not find Paul and Silas, they dragged Jason and some of the other believers before the city authorities, crying, "These people who have turned the world upside down have come here also, ⁷and Jason has received them; and they are all acting against the decrees of Caesar, saying that there is another ruler,⬜ Jesus." ⁸And the people and the city authorities were disturbed when they heard this. ⁹And having taken security from Jason and the rest, the authorities let them go.

¹⁰The community immediately sent Paul and Silas away by night to Beroea; and when they arrived they went into the Jewish synagogue. ¹¹Now these Jews were more noble than those in Thessalonica, for they received the word with all eagerness, examining the scriptures daily to see if these things were so. ¹²Many of them therefore believed, with not a few Greek women of high standing as well as men. ¹³But when the Jews of Thessalonica learned that the word of God was proclaimed by Paul at Beroea also, they came there too, stirring up and inciting the crowds. ¹⁴Then the community immediately sent Paul off on his way to the sea, but Silas and Timothy remained there. ¹⁵Those who conducted Paul brought him as far as Athens; and receiving a command for Silas and Timothy to come to Paul as soon as possible, the two departed.

⬜RSV *king*. See Appendix.

Lesson 1 (alternate) ~ Deuteronomy 6:20-25

These are the statutes that God commanded Israel to keep.

20When your child asks you in time to come, "What is the meaning of the testimonies and the statutes and the ordinances which the SOVEREIGN ONE our God has commanded you?" 21then you shall say to your child, "We were Pharaoh's slaves in Egypt; and GOD brought us out of Egypt with a mighty hand, 22and GOD showed signs and wonders, great and grievous, against Egypt and against Pharaoh and all his household, before our eyes, 23and brought us out from there, in order to bring us in and give us the land which God promised to our ancestors. 24And GOD commanded us to do all these statutes, to fear the SOVEREIGN ONE our God, for our good always, that we might be preserved alive, as at this day. 25And it will be righteousness for us, if we are careful to do all this commandment before the SOVEREIGN ONE our God, as we have been commanded."

Lesson 2 ~ 1 Peter 2:1-10

Christ is the living stone, precious to God.

1So put away all malice and all guile and insincerity and envy and all slander. 2Like newborn babes, long for the pure spiritual milk, that by it you may grow up to salvation; 3for you have tasted the kindness of the Sovereign.□

4Come to Christ, to that living stone, rejected by human beings but in God's sight chosen and precious; 5and like living stones be yourselves built into a spiritual house, to be a holy priesthood, to offer spiritual sacrifices acceptable to God through Jesus Christ. 6For it stands in scripture:

"Behold, I am laying in Zion a stone, a cornerstone chosen and
    precious,
and whoever believes in Christ will not be put to shame."

7The honor, then, is for you who believe, but for those who do not believe,

"The very stone which the builders rejected
    has become the head of the corner,"

8and

"A stone of stumbling,
    and a rock of offense";

for they stumble because they disobey the word, as they were destined to do.

□RSV *Lord.* See Appendix.

⁹But you are a chosen race, a royal priesthood, a holy nation, God's own people, that you may declare the wonderful deeds of God who called you out of the night into God's marvelous light. ¹⁰Once you were no people but now you are God's people; once you had not received mercy but now you have received mercy.

Gospel ~ John 14:1-14

Jesus is the way, the truth, and the life.

¹"Let not your hearts be troubled; believe in God, believe also in me. ²In the house of [*God*] my Father [*and Mother**] are many rooms; if it were not so, would I have told you that I go to prepare a place for you? ³And when I go and prepare a place for you, I will come again and will take you to myself, that where I am you may be also. ⁴And you know the way where I am going." ⁵Thomas said to Jesus, "My Sovereign,▫ we do not know where you are going; how can we know the way?" ⁶Jesus said to Thomas, "I am the way, and the truth, and the life; no one comes to God,⊗ but by me. ⁷If you had known me, you would have known God⊗ also; henceforth you know God and have seen God."

⁸Philip said to Jesus, "My Sovereign,▫ show us God,⊗ and we shall be satisfied." ⁹Jesus said to Philip, "Have I been with you so long, and yet you do not know me, Philip? Whoever has seen me has seen God;⊗ how can you say, 'Show us God'⊗? ¹⁰Do you not believe that I am in God⊗ and God⊗ in me? The words that I say to you I do not speak on my own authority; but God⊗ who dwells in me does God's works. ¹¹Believe me that I am in God⊗ and God⊗ in me; or else believe me for the sake of the works themselves.

¹²"Truly, truly, I say to you, whoever believes in me will also do the works that I do; and greater works than these will the believer do, because I go to God.⊗ ¹³Whatever you ask in my name, I will do it, that [*God*] the Father [*and Mother**] may be glorified in the Child◇ [*of God*]; ¹⁴if you ask anything in my name, I will do it."

---

*Addition to the text. RSV v. 2 *my Father's house;* v. 13 *the Father.* See "Metaphor" and "God the Father and Mother" in the Appendix.
▫RSV *Lord.* See Appendix.
⊗RSV vs. 6, 8, 9, 10, 11, 12 *the Father;* v. 7 *my Father.*
◇RSV *Son.* See Appendix.

EASTER 6

Lesson 1 ~ Acts 17:22-31

Paul preaches to the Athenians.

²²Paul, standing in the middle of the Areopagus, said: "People of Athens, I perceive that in every way you are very religious. ²³For as I passed along, and observed the objects of your worship, I found also an altar with this inscription, 'To an unknown god.' What therefore you worship as unknown, this I proclaim to you. ²⁴The God who made the world and everything in it, being Sovereign□ of heaven and earth, does not live in shrines made by human hands, ²⁵and is not served by human hands, as though God needed anything, since God alone gives to all people life and breath and everything. ²⁶And this God made from one all the nations to live on the face of the whole earth, having determined allotted periods and the boundaries of their habitation, ²⁷that they should seek God, in the hope that they might feel after and find God, who is not far from each one of us, ²⁸for

'In this one we live and move and have our being';
as even some of your poets have said,
'For we are indeed the offspring of God.'

²⁹Being then God's offspring, we ought not to think that the Deity is like gold, or silver, or stone, a representation by human art and imagination. ³⁰The times of ignorance God overlooked, but now God commands all people everywhere to repent, ³¹because the day has been fixed on which God will judge the world in righteousness by a human being whom God has appointed, and of this God has given assurance to all by raising that one from the dead."

Lesson 1 (alternate) ~ Acts 8:4-8, 14-17

Peter and John lay their hands on the Samaritans, who then receive the Holy Spirit.

⁴Now those who were scattered went about preaching the word. ⁵Philip went down to a city of Samaria, and proclaimed to them the Christ. ⁶And the multitudes with one accord gave heed to what was said by Philip, when they heard him and saw the signs which he did. ⁷For unclean spirits came out of many who were possessed, crying with a loud voice; and many who were paralyzed or lame were healed. ⁸So there was much joy in that city. . . .

¹⁴Now when the apostles at Jerusalem heard that Samaria had received

---

□RSV *Lord.* See Appendix.

the word of God, they sent to them Peter and John, ¹⁵who came down and prayed for them that they might receive the Holy Spirit; ¹⁶for it had not yet fallen on any of them, but they had only been baptized in the name of the Sovereign□ Jesus. ¹⁷Then they laid their hands on them and they received the Holy Spirit.

Lesson 1 (alternate) ~ Isaiah 41:17-20

The God of Israel will not forsake the people.

¹⁷When the poor and needy seek water,
    and there is none,
    and their tongue is parched with thirst,
  I the SOVEREIGN ONE will answer them,
    I the God of Israel will not forsake them.
¹⁸I will open rivers on the bare heights,
    and fountains in the midst of the valleys;
  I will make the wilderness a pool of water,
    and the dry land springs of water.
¹⁹I will put in the wilderness the cedar,
    the acacia, the myrtle, and the olive;
  I will set in the desert the cypress,
    the plane and the pine together;
²⁰that all may see and know,
    may consider and understand together,
  that the hand of the SOVEREIGN ONE has done this,
    the Holy One of Israel has created it.

Lesson 2 ~ 1 Peter 3:8-22

We are admonished not to fear suffering for righteousness' sake.

⁸Finally, all of you, have unity of spirit, sympathy, love for one another, a tender heart and a humble mind. ⁹Do not return evil for evil or reviling for reviling; but on the contrary bless, for to this you have been called, that you may obtain a blessing. ¹⁰For
  "All who would love life
  and see good days,
  let them keep their tongues from evil
  and their lips from speaking guile;
¹¹let them turn away from evil and do right;
  let them seek peace and pursue it.

□RSV *Lord.* See Appendix.

¹²For the eyes of the Sovereign One□ are upon the righteous,
and God's ears are open to their prayer.
But the face of the Sovereign One□ is against those that do evil."
¹³Now who is there to harm you if you are zealous for what is right?
¹⁴But even if you do suffer for righteousness' sake, you will be blessed.
Have no fear of them, nor be troubled, ¹⁵but in your hearts reverence
Christ as Sovereign.□ Always be prepared to make a defense to any one who
calls you to account for the hope that is in you, yet do it with gentleness and
reverence; ¹⁶and keep your conscience clear, so that, when you are abused,
those who revile your good behavior in Christ may be put to shame. ¹⁷For it
is better to suffer for doing right, if that should be God's will, than for doing
wrong. ¹⁸For Christ also died for sins once for all, the righteous for the
unrighteous, in order to bring us to God, being put to death in the flesh but
made alive in the spirit; ¹⁹in which Christ went and preached to the spirits
in prison, ²⁰who formerly did not obey, when God's patience waited in the
days of Noah, during the building of the ark, in which a few, that is, eight
persons, were saved through water. ²¹Baptism, which corresponds to this,
now saves you, not as a removal of dirt from the body but as an appeal to
God for a clear conscience, through the resurrection of Jesus Christ, ²²who
has gone into heaven and is at the right hand of God, to rule over angels,
authorities, and powers.

Gospel ~ John 14:15-21

The one who loves Jesus keeps Jesus' commandments.

¹⁵If you love me, you will keep my commandments. ¹⁶And I will pray
[*to God*] the [*Mother and**] Father, who will give you another Counselor,
to be with you for ever, ¹⁷even the Spirit of truth, whom the world cannot
receive, because it neither sees nor knows this Spirit; you know the Spirit,
who dwells with you, and will be in you.

¹⁸I will not leave you desolate; I will come to you. ¹⁹Yet a little while,
and the world will see me no more, but you will see me; because I live, you
will live also. ²⁰In that day you will know that I am in God,⊗ and you in me,
and I in you. ²¹Whoever has my commandments and keeps them, that is
the one who loves me; and all who love me will be loved by God,⊗ and I will
love them and manifest myself to them.

□RSV *Lord.* See Appendix.
*Addition to the text. See "Metaphor" and "God the Father and Mother" in the Appendix.
⊗RSV *my Father.*

ASCENSION

Lesson 1 ~ Acts 1:1-11

The risen Jesus is taken up into heaven.

¹In the first book, O Theophilus, I have dealt with all that Jesus began to do and teach, ²until the day when Jesus was taken up, having given commandment through the Holy Spirit to the apostles whom Jesus had chosen. ³After the passion Jesus was seen alive by the apostles through many proofs, appearing to them during forty days, and speaking of the realm* of God. ⁴And while staying with the apostles, Jesus charged them not to depart from Jerusalem, but to wait for the promise of God, which, Jesus said, "you heard from me, ⁵for John baptized with water, but before many days you shall be baptized with the Holy Spirit."

⁶So when the apostles had come together, they asked Jesus, "Our Sovereign,□ will you at this time restore the realm* to Israel?" ⁷Jesus said, "It is not for you to know times or seasons which have been fixed by God's own authority. ⁸But you shall receive power when the Holy Spirit has come upon you; and you shall be my witnesses in Jerusalem and in all Judea and Samaria and to the end of the earth." ⁹And having said this, as the apostles were looking on, Jesus was lifted up and carried on a cloud out of their sight. ¹⁰And while they were gazing into heaven as Jesus went, two figures stood by them in white robes, ¹¹and said, "People of Galilee, why do you stand looking into heaven? This Jesus, who was taken up from you into heaven, will come in the same way as you saw Jesus go into heaven."

Lesson 1 (alternate) ~ Daniel 7:9-14

One like a human one comes to the Ancient of Days.

⁹As I looked,
>   thrones were placed
>   and one that was ancient of days sat down,
>   whose raiment was white as snow,
>   and whose hair was like pure wool;
>   whose throne was fiery flames,
>   its wheels were burning fire.

---

*RSV *kingdom*. See Appendix.
□RSV *Lord*. See Appendix.

¹⁰A stream of fire issued
    and came forth from before the ancient of days,
who was served by a thousand thousands,
    and before whom stood ten thousand times ten thousand;
the court sat in judgment,
    and the books were opened.
¹¹I looked then because of the sound of the great words which the horn was speaking. And as I looked, the beast was slain, and its body destroyed and given over to be burned with fire. ¹²As for the rest of the beasts, their dominion was taken away, but their lives were prolonged for a season and a time. ¹³I saw in the night visions,
    and behold, with the clouds of heaven
        there came one like a human one,°
who came to the Ancient of Days
    and was presented before the Ancient of Days.
¹⁴And to that one was given dominion,
    and glory and sovereignty,
that all peoples, nations, and languages
    should serve that one,
whose dominion is an everlasting dominion,
    which shall not pass away,
and whose realm* is one
    that shall not be destroyed.

Lesson 2 ~ Ephesians 1:15-23

The risen Christ is exalted as head of all.

¹⁵For this reason, because I have heard of your faith in the Sovereign□ Jesus and your love toward all the saints, ¹⁶I do not cease to give thanks for you, remembering you in my prayers, ¹⁷that the God of our Sovereign□ Jesus Christ, the Father [*and Mother**] of glory, may give you a spirit of wisdom and of revelation in the knowledge of God, ¹⁸having the eyes of your hearts enlightened, that you may know what is the hope to which you have been called, what are the riches of God's glorious inheritance in the saints, ¹⁹and what is the immeasurable greatness of God's power in us who believe, according to the working of God's great might ²⁰which was accomplished in Christ when God raised Christ from the dead and made Christ sit at the right hand in the heavenly places, ²¹far above all rule and

---

°RSV *son of man.* See Appendix.
*RSV *kingdom.* See Appendix.
□RSV *Lord.* See Appendix.
*Addition to the text. See "Metaphor" and "God the Father and Mother" in the Appendix.

authority and power and dominion, and above every name that is named, not only in this age but also in that which is to come; ²²and God has put all things under Christ's feet and has made Christ the head over all things for the church, ²³which is the body of Christ, the fulness of the one who fills all in all.

Gospel ~ Matthew 28:16-20

The disciples are commissioned to make disciples, to baptize, and to teach.

¹⁶Now the eleven disciples went to Galilee, to the mountain to which Jesus had directed them. ¹⁷And when they saw Jesus they worshiped him; but some doubted. ¹⁸And Jesus came and said to them, "All authority in heaven and on earth has been given to me. ¹⁹Go therefore and make disciples of all nations, baptizing them in the name of [*God*] the Father [*and Mother**], and of Jesus Christ the beloved Child of God◇ and of the Holy Spirit, ²⁰teaching them to observe all that I have commanded you; and lo, I am with you always, to the close of the age."

Gospel (alternate) ~ Luke 24:44-53

Jesus commissions the disciples and is parted from them.

⁴⁴Then Jesus said to them, "These are my words which I spoke to you, while I was still with you, that everything written about me in the law of Moses and the prophets and the psalms must be fulfilled." ⁴⁵Then Jesus opened their minds to understand the scriptures, ⁴⁶and said to them, "Thus it is written, that the Christ should suffer and on the third day rise from the dead, ⁴⁷and that repentance and forgiveness of sins should be preached in Christ's name to all nations, beginning from Jerusalem. ⁴⁸You are witnesses of these things. ⁴⁹And behold, I send upon you the promise of [*God*] my Father [*and Mother**]; but stay in the city, until you are clothed with power from on high."

⁵⁰Then Jesus led them out as far as Bethany, and with uplifted hands blessed them. ⁵¹While blessing them, Jesus parted from them, and was carried up into heaven. ⁵²And they returned to Jerusalem with great joy, ⁵³and were continually in the temple blessing God.

---

*Addition to the text. See "Metaphor" and "God the Father and Mother" in the Appendix.
◇RSV *and of the Son*. See Appendix.

EASTER 7

Lesson 1 ~ Acts 1:1-14

The risen Jesus is taken up into heaven.

¹In the first book, O Theophilus, I have dealt with all that Jesus began to do and teach, ²until the day when Jesus was taken up, having given commandment through the Holy Spirit to the apostles whom Jesus had chosen. ³After the passion Jesus was seen alive by the apostles through many proofs, appearing to them during forty days, and speaking of the realm* of God. ⁴And while staying with the apostles, Jesus charged them not to depart from Jerusalem, but to wait for the promise of God, which, Jesus said, "you heard from me, ⁵for John baptized with water, but before many days you shall be baptized with the Holy Spirit."

⁶So when the apostles had come together, they asked Jesus, "Our Sovereign,□ will you at this time restore the realm* to Israel?" ⁷Jesus said, "It is not for you to know times or seasons which have been fixed by God's own authority. ⁸But you shall receive power when the Holy Spirit has come upon you; and you shall be my witnesses in Jerusalem and in all Judea and Samaria and to the end of the earth." ⁹And having said this, as the apostles were looking on, Jesus was lifted up and carried on a cloud out of their sight. ¹⁰And while they were gazing into heaven as Jesus went, two figures stood by them in white robes, ¹¹and said, "People of Galilee, why do you stand looking into heaven? This Jesus, who was taken up from you into heaven, will come in the same way as you saw Jesus go into heaven."

¹²Then the apostles returned to Jerusalem from the mount called Olivet, which is near Jerusalem, a sabbath day's journey away; ¹³and when they had entered, they went up to the upper room, where they were staying, Peter and John and James and Andrew, Philip and Thomas, Bartholomew and Matthew, James the son of Alphaeus and Simon the Zealot and Judas the son of James. ¹⁴All these with one accord devoted themselves to prayer, together with the women and Mary the mother of Jesus, and with Jesus' brothers.

---

*RSV *kingdom.* See Appendix.
□RSV *Lord.* See Appendix.

Lesson 1 (alternate) ~ Ezekiel 39:21-29

God's enemies are destroyed, and exiled Israel is restored.

²¹And I will set my glory among the nations; and all the nations shall see my judgment which I have executed, and my hand which I have laid on them. ²²The house of Israel shall know that I am the SOVEREIGN ONE their God, from that day forward. ²³And the nations shall know that the house of Israel went into captivity for their iniquity, because they dealt so treacherously with me that I hid my face from them and gave them into the hand of their adversaries, and they all fell by the sword. ²⁴I dealt with them according to their uncleanness and their transgressions, and hid my face from them.

²⁵Therefore thus says the Sovereign GOD: Now I will restore the fortunes of the house of Jacob, and have mercy upon the whole house of Israel; and I will be jealous for my holy name. ²⁶Israel shall forget their shame, and all the treachery they have practiced against me, when they dwell securely in their land with none to make them afraid, ²⁷when I have brought Israel back from the peoples and gathered them from their enemies' lands, and through them have vindicated my holiness in the sight of many nations. ²⁸Then Israel shall know that I am the SOVEREIGN ONE their GOD because I sent them into exile among the nations, and then gathered them into their own land. I will leave none of them remaining among the nations any more; ²⁹and I will not hide my face any more from them, when I pour out my Spirit upon the house of Israel, says the Sovereign GOD.

Lesson 2 ~ 1 Peter 4:12-19

Those suffering persecution are to do right.

¹²Beloved, do not be surprised at the fiery ordeal which comes upon you to prove you, as though something strange were happening to you. ¹³But rejoice in so far as you share Christ's sufferings, that you may also rejoice and be glad when Christ's glory is revealed. ¹⁴If you are reproached for the name of Christ, you are blessed, because the spirit of glory and of God rests upon you. ¹⁵But let none of you suffer as a murderer, or a thief, or a wrongdoer, or a mischief-maker; ¹⁶yet if any one of you suffers as a Christian, do not be ashamed, but under that name glorify God. ¹⁷For the time has come for judgment to begin with the household of God; and if it begins with us, what will be the end of those who do not obey the gospel of God? ¹⁸And

"If one who is righteous is scarcely saved,
    where will the impious and sinner appear?"

¹⁹Therefore let those who suffer according to God's will do what is right and entrust their souls to a faithful Creator.

Gospel ~ John 17:1-11

Jesus prays for the disciples.

¹Having spoken these words, Jesus looked up to heaven and said, "[*God my Mother and**] Father, the hour has come; glorify your Child° that your Child° may glorify you, ²since you have given that Child power over all flesh, to give eternal life to all whom you have given your Child. ³And this is eternal life, that they know you the only true God, and Jesus Christ whom you have sent. ⁴I glorified you on earth, having accomplished the work which you gave me to do; ⁵and now, [*God my*] Father [*and Mother**], glorify me in your own presence with the glory which I had with you before the world was made.

⁶"I have manifested your name to those whom you gave me out of the world; yours they were, and you gave them to me, and they have kept your word. ⁷Now they know that everything that you have given me is from you; ⁸for I have given them the words which you gave me, and they have received them and know in truth that I came from you; and they have believed that you sent me. ⁹I am praying for them; I am not praying for the world but for those whom you have given me, for they are yours; ¹⁰all mine are yours, and yours are mine, and I am glorified in them. ¹¹And now I am no more in the world, but they are in the world, and I am coming to you. Holy [*God my Mother and**] Father, keep them in your name, which you have given me, that they may be one, even as we are one."

---

*Addition to the text. See "Metaphor" and "God the Father and Mother" in the Appendix.
°RSV *Son*. See Appendix.

PENTECOST 1

Lesson 1 ~ Joel 2:28-32

The Spirit is poured out on the day of God.

²⁸And it shall come to pass afterward,
    that I will pour out my spirit on all flesh;
  your sons and your daughters shall prophesy,
    the old shall dream dreams,
    and the young shall see visions.
²⁹Even upon the menservants and maidservants
    in those days, I will pour out my spirit.

³⁰And I will give portents in the heavens and on the earth, blood and fire and columns of smoke. ³¹The sun shall be turned to night, and the moon to blood, before the great and terrible day of GOD comes. ³²And it shall come to pass that all who call upon the name of GOD shall be delivered; for in Mount Zion and in Jerusalem there shall be those who escape, as GOD has said, and among the survivors shall be those whom GOD calls.

Lesson 2 ~ Acts 2:1-21

Luke describes the day of Pentecost when worshipers are filled with the Holy Spirit, and Peter preaches.

¹When the day of Pentecost had come, they were all together in one place. ²And suddenly a sound came from heaven like the rush of a mighty wind, and it filled all the house where they were sitting. ³And there appeared to them tongues as of fire, distributed and resting on each one of them. ⁴And they were all filled with the Holy Spirit and began to speak in other tongues, as the Spirit gave them utterance.

⁵Now there were dwelling in Jerusalem devout Jews from every nation under heaven. ⁶And at this sound the multitude came together, and they were bewildered, because they heard them speaking in their own language. ⁷And they were amazed and wondered, saying, "Are not all these who are speaking Galileans? ⁸And how is it that we hear, each of us in our own native language? ⁹Parthians and Medes and Elamites and residents of Mesopotamia, Judea and Cappadocia, Pontus and Asia, ¹⁰Phrygia and Pamphylia, Egypt and the parts of Libya belonging to Cyrene, and visitors from Rome, both Jews and proselytes, ¹¹Cretans and Arabians, we hear them telling in our own tongues the mighty works of God." ¹²And all were amazed and perplexed, saying to one another, "What does this mean?" ¹³But others mocking said, "They are filled with new wine."

¹⁴But Peter, standing with the eleven, lifted up his voice and addressed them, "People of Judea and all who dwell in Jerusalem, let this be known to you, and give ear to my words. ¹⁵For these people are not drunk, as you suppose, since it is only the third hour of the day; ¹⁶but this is what was spoken by the prophet Joel:

¹⁷'And in the last days it shall be, God declares,
    that I will pour out my Spirit upon all flesh,
    and your sons and your daughters shall prophesy,
    and the young shall see visions,
    and the old shall dream dreams;
¹⁸yea, and on my menservants and my maidservants in those days
    I will pour out my Spirit; and they shall prophesy.
¹⁹And I will show wonders in the heaven above
    and signs on the earth beneath,
    blood, and fire, and vapor of smoke;
²⁰the sun shall be turned into night
    and the moon into blood,
    before the day of the Sovereign One□ comes,
    the great and manifest day.
²¹And it shall be that whoever calls on the name of the Sovereign One□
        shall be saved.' "

Gospel ~ John 20:19-23

Jesus breathes the Spirit upon the disciples.

¹⁹On the evening of that day, the first day of the week, the doors being shut where the disciples were, for fear of the Jewish authorities, Jesus came and stood among them and said to them, "Peace be with you." ²⁰Having said this, Jesus showed them his hands and side. Then the disciples were glad when they saw the Sovereign.□ ²¹Jesus said to them again, "Peace be with you. As [God] the [Mother and*] Father has sent me, even so I send you." ²²Having said this, Jesus breathed on them, and said to them, "Receive the Holy Spirit. ²³If you forgive the sins of any, they are forgiven; if you retain the sins of any, they are retained."

─────────────

□RSV *Lord.* See Appendix.
*Addition to the text. See "Metaphor" and "God the Father and Mother" in the Appendix.

TRINITY

God creates the world and all its inhabitants.

[1]In the beginning God created the heavens and the earth. [2]The earth was without form and void, and darkness was upon the face of the deep; and the Spirit of God was moving over the face of the waters.

[3]And God said, "Let there be light"; and there was light. [4]And God saw that the light was good; and God separated the light from the darkness. [5]God called the light Day, and the darkness Night. And there was evening and there was morning, one day.

[6]And God said, "Let there be a firmament in the midst of the waters, and let it separate the waters from the waters." [7]And God made the firmament and separated the waters which were under the firmament from the waters which were above the firmament. And it was so. [8]And God called the firmament Heaven. And there was evening and there was morning, a second day.

[9]And God said, "Let the waters under the heavens be gathered together into one place, and let the dry land appear." And it was so. [10]God called the dry land Earth, and the waters that were gathered together God called Seas. And God saw that it was good. [11]And God said, "Let the earth put forth vegetation, plants yielding seed, and fruit trees bearing fruit in which is their seed, each according to its kind, upon the earth." And it was so. [12]The earth brought forth vegetation, plants yielding seed according to their own kinds, and trees bearing fruit in which is their seed, each according to its kind. And God saw that it was good. [13]And there was evening and there was morning, a third day.

[14]And God said, "Let there be lights in the firmament of the heavens to separate the day from the night; and let them be for signs and for seasons and for days and years, [15]and let them be lights in the firmament of the heavens to give light upon the earth." And it was so. [16]And God made the two great lights, the greater light to rule the day, and the lesser light to rule the night; God made the stars also. [17]And God set them in the firmament of the heavens to give light upon the earth, [18]to rule over the day and over the night, and to separate the light from the darkness. And God saw that it was good. [19]And there was evening and there was morning, a fourth day.

[20]And God said, "Let the waters bring forth swarms of living creatures, and let birds fly above the earth across the firmament of the heavens." [21]So God created the great sea monsters and every living creature that moves, with which the waters swarm, according to their kinds, and every winged bird according to its kind. And God saw that it was good. [22]And God blessed them, saying, "Be fruitful and multiply and fill the waters in the seas, and let birds multiply on the earth." [23]And there was evening and there was morning, a fifth day.

[24]And God said, "Let the earth bring forth living creatures according to their kinds: cattle and creeping things and beasts of the earth according to their kinds." And it was so. [25]And God made the beasts of the earth according to their kinds and the cattle according to their kinds, and

everything that creeps upon the ground according to its kind. And God saw that it was good.

26Then God said, "Let us make humankind in our image, after our likeness; and let them have dominion over the fish of the sea, and over the birds of the air, and over the cattle, and over all the earth, and over every creeping thing that creeps upon the earth." 27So God created humankind in God's own image, in the image of God was the human being created; male and female God created them. 28And God blessed them, and God said to them, "Be fruitful and multiply, and fill the earth and subdue it; and have dominion over the fish of the sea and over the birds of the air and over every living thing that moves upon the earth." 29And God said, "Behold, I have given you every plant yielding seed which is upon the face of all the earth, and every tree with seed in its fruit; you shall have them for food. 30And to every beast of the earth, and to every bird of the air, and to everything that creeps on the earth, everything that has the breath of life, I have given every green plant for food." And it was so. 31And God saw everything that was made, and behold, it was very good. And there was evening and there was morning, a sixth day.

2:1Thus the heavens and the earth were finished, and all the host of them. 2And on the seventh day God finished the work which God had done, and on the seventh day rested from all the work which God had done. 3So God blessed the seventh day and hallowed it, because on it God rested from all the work which God had done in creation.

Lesson 2 ~ 2 Corinthians 13:5-14

Paul exhorts the church at Corinth.

5Examine yourselves, to see whether you are holding to your faith. Test yourselves. Do you not realize that Jesus Christ is in you?—unless indeed you fail to meet the test! 6I hope you will find out that we have not failed. 7But we pray God that you may not do wrong—not that we may appear to have met the test, but that you may do what is right, though we may seem to have failed. 8For we cannot do anything against the truth, but only for the truth. 9For we are glad when we are weak and you are strong. What we pray for is your improvement. 10I write this while I am away from you, in order that when I come I may not have to be severe in my use of the authority which the Sovereign□ has given me for building up and not for tearing down.

11Finally, my friends, farewell. Mend your ways, heed my appeal, agree with one another, live in peace, and the God of love and peace will be with you. 12Greet one another with a holy kiss. 13All the saints greet you.

14The grace of the Sovereign□ Jesus Christ and the love of God and the communion of the Holy Spirit be with you all.

Gospel ~ Matthew 28:16-20

See Ascension, Gospel

□RSV *Lord.* See Appendix.

PENTECOST 2

Lesson 1 ~ Deuteronomy 11:18-21, 26-28

A blessing and a curse are set before Israel.

¹⁸You shall therefore lay up these words of mine in your heart and in your soul; and you shall bind them as a sign upon your hand, and they shall be as frontlets between your eyes. ¹⁹And you shall teach them to your children, talking of them when you are sitting in your house, and when you are walking by the way, and when you lie down, and when you rise. ²⁰And you shall write them upon the doorposts of your house and upon your gates, ²¹that your days and the days of your children may be multiplied in the land which GOD swore to your ancestors to give them, as long as the heavens are above the earth. . . .

²⁶Behold, I set before you this day a blessing and a curse: ²⁷the blessing, if you obey the commandments of the SOVEREIGN ONE your God, which I command you this day, ²⁸and the curse, if you do not obey the commandments of the SOVEREIGN ONE your God, but turn aside from the way which I command you this day, to go after other gods which you have not known.

Lesson 2 ~ Romans 3:21-28

Righteousness is based on faith, not on works.

²¹But now the righteousness of God has been manifested apart from law, although the law and the prophets bear witness to it, ²²the righteousness of God through faith in Jesus Christ for all who believe. For there is no distinction; ²³since all have sinned and fall short of the glory of God, ²⁴they are justified by God's grace as a gift, through the redemption which is in Christ Jesus, ²⁵whom God put forward as a blood expiation, to be received by faith. This was to show God's righteousness, because in divine forbearance God had passed over former sins; ²⁶it was to prove at the present time that God is indeed righteous and justifies one who has faith in Jesus.

²⁷Then what becomes of our boasting? It is excluded. On what principle? On the principle of works? No, but on the principle of faith. ²⁸For we hold that one is justified by faith apart from works of law.

Jesus tells the parable of a house built on the rock and a house built on the sand.

¹⁵"Beware of false prophets, who come to you in sheep's clothing but inwardly are ravenous wolves. ¹⁶You will know them by their fruits. Are grapes gathered from thorns, or figs from thistles? ¹⁷So, every sound tree bears good fruit, but the bad tree bears evil fruit. ¹⁸A sound tree cannot bear evil fruit, nor can a bad tree bear good fruit. ¹⁹Every tree that does not bear good fruit is cut down and thrown into the fire. ²⁰Thus you will know them by their fruits.

²¹"Not every one who says to me, 'My Sovereign, my Sovereign,'□ shall enter the realm* of heaven, but those who do the will of [*God*] my Father [*and Mother**] who is in heaven. ²²On that day many will say to me, 'My Sovereign, my Sovereign,□ did we not prophesy in your name, and cast out demons in your name, and do many mighty works in your name?' ²³And then will I declare to them, 'I never knew you; depart from me, you evildoers.'

²⁴"Every one then who hears these words of mine and does them will be like someone wise enough to build a house upon the rock; ²⁵and the rain fell, and the floods came, and the winds blew and beat upon that house, but it did not fall, because it had been founded on the rock. ²⁶And every one who hears these words of mine and does not do them will be like the fool who built a house upon the sand; ²⁷and the rain fell, and the floods came, and the winds blew and beat against that house, and it fell; and great was the fall of it."

²⁸And when Jesus finished these sayings, the crowds were astonished at his teaching, ²⁹for Jesus taught them as one who had authority, and not as their scribes.

□RSV *Lord, Lord.* See Appendix.
*RSV *kingdom.* See Appendix.
*Addition to the text. See "Metaphor" and "God the Father and Mother" in the Appendix.

PENTECOST 3

Lesson 1 ~ Hosea 5:15–6:6

When Ephraim, or Israel, was wounded, the God of Ephraim spoke.

¹⁵I will return again to my place,
until they acknowledge their guilt and seek my face,
and in their distress they seek me, saying,
^{6:1}"Come, let us return to GOD:
who has torn, that we may be healed;
who has stricken and will bind us up.
²After two days God will revive us;
on the third day God will raise us up,
that we may live in the presence of God.
³Let us know, let us press on to know GOD;
God's going forth is sure as the dawn;
God will come to us as the showers,
as the spring rains that water the earth."
⁴What shall I do with you, O Ephraim?
What shall I do with you, O Judah?
Your love is like a morning cloud,
like the dew that goes early away.
⁵Therefore I have hewn them by the prophets,
I have slain them by the words of my mouth,
and my judgment goes forth as the light.
⁶For I desire steadfast love and not sacrifice,
the knowledge of God, rather than burnt offerings.

Lesson 2 ~ Romans 4:13-25

Paul writes that everything depends on faith—not on what one does, but on the grace of God.

¹³The promise to Abraham [*and Sarah**] and their descendants, that they should inherit the world, did not come through the law but through the righteousness of faith. ¹⁴If it is the adherents of the law who are to be heirs, faith is null and the promise is void. ¹⁵For the law brings wrath, but where there is no law there is no transgression.
¹⁶That is why it depends on faith, in order that the promise may rest on

---

*Addition to the text. See Appendix.

grace and be guaranteed to all their descendants—not only to the adherents of the law but also to those who share the faith of Abraham [*and Sarah**], who are the ancestors of us all, [17]as it is written, "I have made you the ancestors of many nations"—in the presence of the God in whom Abraham [*and Sarah**] believed, who gives life to the dead and calls into existence the things that do not exist. [18]In hope Abraham [*and Sarah**] believed against hope, that they should become the ancestors of many nations; as they had been told, "So shall your descendants be." [19]They did not weaken in faith when they considered their own bodies, which were as good as dead because they were about a hundred years old, or when they considered the barrenness of Sarah's womb. [20]No distrust made them waver concerning the promise of God, but they grew strong in their faith as they gave glory to God, [21]fully convinced that God was able to do what God had promised. [22]That is why their faith was "reckoned to them as righteousness." [23]But the words, "it was reckoned to them," were written not for their sake alone, [24]but for ours also. It will be reckoned to us who believe in God who raised from the dead Jesus our Sovereign,□ [25]who was put to death for our trespasses and raised for our justification.

Gospel ~ Matthew 9:9-13

Jesus calls a tax collector as a disciple, and announces that he goes not to those who are well but to those who are sick.

[9]Passing on from there, Jesus saw someone called Matthew sitting at the tax office; and Jesus said to Matthew, "Follow me." And Matthew rose and followed Jesus.

[10]And as Jesus sat at table in the house, behold, many tax collectors and sinners came and sat down with Jesus and the disciples. [11]And when the Pharisees saw this, they said to the disciples, "Why does your teacher eat with tax collectors and sinners?" [12]But hearing this, Jesus said, "Those who are well have no need of a physician, but those who are sick. [13]Go and learn what this means, 'I desire mercy, and not sacrifice.' For I came not to call the righteous, but sinners."

---

*Addition to the text. See Appendix.
□ RSV *Lord*. See Appendix.

PENTECOST 4

Lesson 1 ~ Exodus 19:2-8a

Israel has left the land of Egypt and comes into the wilderness of Sinai.

²And when the people of Israel set out from Rephidim and came into the wilderness of Sinai, they encamped in the wilderness; and there Israel encamped before the mountain. ³And Moses went up to God, and GOD called to Moses out of the mountain, saying, "Thus you shall say to the house of Jacob, and tell the people of Israel: ⁴You have seen what I did to the Egyptians, and how I bore you on eagles' wings and brought you to myself. ⁵Now therefore, if you will obey my voice and keep my covenant, you shall be my own possession among all peoples; for all the earth is mine, ⁶and you shall be to me a priestly people and a holy nation. These are the words which you shall speak to the children of Israel."

⁷So Moses came and called the elders of the people, and set before them all these words which GOD had commanded. ⁸And all the people answered together and said, "All that GOD has spoken we will do."

Lesson 2 ~ Romans 5:6-11

Having just spoken of God's great love which has been poured into our hearts through the Holy Spirit, Paul continues:

⁶While we were still weak, at the right time Christ died for the ungodly. ⁷Why, one will hardly die for a righteous person—though perhaps for good people one will dare even to die. ⁸But God shows love for us in that while we were yet sinners Christ died for us. ⁹Since, therefore, we are now justified by the blood of Christ, much more shall we be saved by Christ from the wrath of God. ¹⁰For if while we were enemies we were reconciled to God by the death of God's Child,° much more, now that we are reconciled, shall we be saved by the life of Christ. ¹¹Not only so, but we also rejoice in God through our Sovereign□ Jesus Christ, through whom we have now received our reconciliation.

°RSV *of his Son*. See Appendix.
□RSV *Lord*. See Appendix.

Matthew narrates Jesus' calling of the twelve disciples and Jesus' charge to them when they are sent out.

³⁵And Jesus went about all the cities and villages, teaching in their synagogues and preaching the gospel of the realm of God,** and healing every disease and every infirmity. ³⁶Seeing the crowds, Jesus had compassion for them, because they were harassed and helpless, like sheep without a shepherd. ³⁷Then Jesus said to the disciples, "The harvest is plentiful, but the laborers are few; ³⁸pray therefore to the God who gives the harvest to send out laborers into the harvest."

^{10:1}And Jesus summoned the twelve disciples and gave them authority over unclean spirits, to cast them out, and to heal every disease and every infirmity. ²The names of the twelve apostles are these: first, Simon, who is called Peter, and Andrew his brother; James the son of Zebedee, and John his brother; ³Philip and Bartholomew; Thomas and Matthew the tax collector; James the son of Alphaeus, and Thaddaeus; ⁴Simon the Cananaean, and Judas Iscariot, who betrayed Jesus.

⁵These twelve Jesus sent out, charging them, "Go nowhere among the Gentiles, and enter no town of the Samaritans, ⁶but go rather to the lost sheep of the house of Israel. ⁷And preach as you go, saying, 'The realm* of heaven is at hand.' ⁸Heal the sick, raise the dead, cleanse lepers, cast out demons. You received without paying, give without pay. ⁹Take no gold, nor silver, nor copper in your belts, ¹⁰no bag for your journey, nor two tunics, nor sandals, nor a staff; for laborers deserve their food. ¹¹And whatever town or village you enter, find out who is worthy in it, and stay there until you depart. ¹²As you enter the house, salute it. ¹³And if the house is worthy, let your peace come upon it; but if it is not worthy, let your peace return to you. ¹⁴And if any one will not receive you or listen to your words, shake off the dust from your feet as you leave that house or town. ¹⁵Truly, I say to you, it shall be more tolerable on the day of judgment for the land of Sodom and Gomorrah than for that town."

**The phrase *gospel of the kingdom* is peculiar to Matthew (4:23; 9:35; 24:14). In each of these cases it is presented in this lectionary as "gospel of the realm of God."
*RSV *kingdom*. See Appendix.

PENTECOST 5

Lesson 1 ~ Jeremiah 20:7-13

Jeremiah feels a compulsion to speak for God, and is denounced by the people.

⁷O GOD, you have deceived me,
  and I was deceived;
you are stronger than I,
  and you have prevailed.
I have become a laughingstock all the day;
  every one mocks me.
⁸For whenever I speak, I cry out,
  I shout, "Violence and destruction!"
For the word of GOD has become for me
  a reproach and derision all day long.
⁹If I say, "I will not mention God,
  or speak any more in God's name,"
there is in my heart as it were a burning fire
  shut up in my bones,
and I am weary with holding it in,
  and I cannot.
¹⁰For I hear many whispering.
  Terror is on every side!
"Denounce him! Let us denounce Jeremiah!"
  say all my familiar friends,
  watching for my fall.
"Perhaps he will be deceived,
  then we can overcome Jeremiah,
  and take our revenge on Jeremiah."
¹¹But GOD is with me as a dread warrior;
  therefore my persecutors will stumble,
  they will not overcome me.
They will be greatly shamed,
  for they will not succeed.
Their eternal dishonor
  will never be forgotten.
¹²O GOD of hosts, you try the righteous,
  you see the heart and the mind,
let me see your vengeance upon them,
  for to you have I committed my cause.
¹³Sing to GOD;
  praise GOD!
For God has delivered the life of the needy
  from the hand of evildoers.

Lesson 2 ~ Romans 5:12-21

See Lent 1, Lesson 2

Gospel ~ Matthew 10:16-33

Jesus tells the disciples that they will be treated shamefully by the world, but that they should have nothing to fear.

¹⁶Behold, I send you out as sheep in the midst of wolves; so be wise as serpents and innocent as doves. ¹⁷Beware of some people; for they will deliver you up to councils, and flog you in their synagogues, ¹⁸and you will be dragged before governors and rulers for my sake, to bear testimony before them and the Gentiles. ¹⁹When they deliver you up, do not be anxious how you are to speak or what you are to say; for what you are to say will be given to you in that hour; ²⁰for it is not you who speak, but the Spirit of God⊗ speaking through you. ²¹Brothers and sisters will deliver up each other to death, and parents their children, and children will rise against parents and have them put to death; ²²and you will be hated by all for my name's sake. But whoever endures to the end will be saved. ²³When they persecute you in one town, flee to the next; for truly, I say to you, you will not have gone through all the towns of Israel, before the Human One° comes.

²⁴A disciple is not above the teacher, nor a servant above the one who is served; ²⁵it is enough for the disciple to be like the teacher, and the servant like the one who is served. If they have called the householder Beelzebul, how much more will they malign those of that household.

²⁶So have no fear of them; for nothing is covered that will not be revealed, or hidden that will not be known. ²⁷What I tell you in the dark, utter in the light; and what you hear whispered, proclaim upon the housetops. ²⁸And do not fear those who kill the body but cannot kill the soul; rather fear the one who can destroy both soul and body in hell. ²⁹Are not two sparrows sold for a penny? And not one of them will fall to the ground without the will of God.⊗ ³⁰But even the hairs of your head are all numbered. ³¹Fear not, therefore; you are of more value than many sparrows. ³²So every one who acknowledges me before others, I also will acknowledge before [God] my [Mother and*] Father who is in heaven; ³³but whoever denies me before others, I also will deny before [God] my Father [and Mother*] who is in heaven.

⊗RSV v. 20 *your Father;* v. 29 *your Father's will.*
°RSV *Son of man.* See Appendix.
*Addition to the text. See "Metaphor" and "God the Father and Mother" in the Appendix.

PENTECOST 6

Lesson 1 ~ 2 Kings 4:8-16

Hear the story of Elisha and the Shunammite woman.

⁸One day Elisha went on to Shunem, where a wealthy woman lived, who urged him to eat some food. So whenever Elisha passed that way, he would turn in there to eat food. ⁹And she said to her husband, "Behold now, I perceive that this is a holy man of God, who is continually passing our way. ¹⁰Let us make a small roof chamber with walls, and put there for him a bed, a table, a chair, and a lamp, so that whenever Elisha comes to us, he can go in there."

¹¹One day Elisha came there, and turned into the chamber and rested there. ¹²And he said to Gehazi his servant, "Call this Shunammite." When Gehazi had called her, she stood before him. ¹³Elisha said to Gehazi, "Say now to her, See, you have taken all this trouble for us; what is to be done for you? Would you have a word spoken on your behalf to the ruler or to the commander of the army?" She answered, "I dwell among my own people." ¹⁴And Elisha said, "What then is to be done for her?" Gehazi answered, "Well, she has no heir, and her husband is old." ¹⁵Elisha said, "Call her." And when Gehazi had called her, she stood in the doorway. ¹⁶And Elisha said, "At this season, when the time comes round, you shall embrace an heir." And she said, "No, my lord,** O servant of God; do not lie to your servant."

Lesson 2 ~ Romans 6:1-11

Having just written that where sin increases, grace abounds, Paul continues now to speak of one's life in Christ.

¹What shall we say then? Are we to continue in sin that grace may abound? ²By no means! How can we who died to sin still live in it? ³Do you not know that all of us who have been baptized into Christ Jesus were baptized into Christ's death? ⁴We were buried therefore with Christ by baptism into death, so that as Christ was raised from the dead by the glory of [God] the Father [and Mother*], we too might walk in newness of life.

⁵For if we have been united with Christ in a death like that, we shall

---

**Designation of respect in the context of this passage; recognized as classist in contemporary society.
*Addition to the text. See "Metaphor" and "God the Father and Mother" in the Appendix.

certainly be united with Christ in a resurrection like that. ⁶We know that our old self was crucified with Christ so that the sinful body might be destroyed, and we might no longer be enslaved to sin. ⁷For any one who has died is freed from sin. ⁸But if we have died with Christ, we believe that we shall also live with Christ. ⁹For we know that Christ being raised from the dead will never die again; death no longer has dominion over Christ. ¹⁰The death Christ died Christ died to sin, once for all, but the life Christ lives Christ lives to God. ¹¹So you also must consider yourselves dead to sin and alive to God in Christ Jesus.

Gospel ~ Matthew 10:34-42

Jesus' coming into the world divides people from each other: some take up the cross, and some do not.

³⁴Do not think that I have come to bring peace on earth; I have not come to bring peace, but a sword. ³⁵For I have come to set a man against his father, and a daughter against her mother, and a daughter-in-law against her mother-in-law; ³⁶and one's foes will be those of one's own household. ³⁷Whoever loves father or mother more than me is not worthy of me; and whoever loves son or daughter more than me is not worthy of me; ³⁸and those who do not take their own cross and follow me are not worthy of me. ³⁹Those who find their life will lose it, and those who lose their life for my sake will find it.

⁴⁰Any one who receives you receives me, and any one who receives me receives God who sent me. ⁴¹Any one who receives a prophet because that one is a prophet shall receive the reward of a prophet, and any one who receives the righteous because they are righteous shall receive the reward of a righteous person. ⁴²And whoever gives to one of these little ones even a cup of cold water because that little one is a disciple, truly, I say to you, the giver shall not go unrewarded.

PENTECOST 7

Lesson 1 ~ Zechariah 9:9-13

The prophet Zechariah bids Jerusalem to rejoice, for its Sovereign comes to it.

⁹Rejoice greatly, O daughter Zion!
  Shout aloud, O daughter Jerusalem!
Lo, your ruler[□] comes to you;
  triumphant and victorious,
humble and riding on an ass,
  on a colt the foal of an ass.
¹⁰I will cut off the chariot from Ephraim
  and the war horse from Jerusalem;
and the battle bow shall be cut off,
  and your ruler shall command peace to the nations
and shall reign from sea to sea,
  and from the River to the ends of the earth.
¹¹As for you also, because of the blood of my covenant with you,
  I will set your captives free from the waterless pit.
¹²Return to your stronghold, O prisoners of hope;
  today I declare that I will restore to you double.
¹³For I have bent Judah as my bow;
  I have made Ephraim its arrow.
I will brandish your soldiers, O Zion,
  over your soldiers, O Greece,
  and wield you like a warrior's sword.

Lesson 2 ~ Romans 7:15–8:13

Paul speaks of sin and the law, and of freedom from condemnation in Christ Jesus.

¹⁵I do not understand my own actions. For I do not do what I want, but I do the very thing I hate. ¹⁶Now if I do what I do not want, I agree that the law is good. ¹⁷So then it is no longer I that do it, but sin which dwells within me. ¹⁸For I know that nothing good dwells within me, that is, in my flesh. I can will what is right, but I cannot do it. ¹⁹For I do not do the good I want, but the evil I do not want is what I do. ²⁰Now if I do what I do not want, it is no longer I that do it, but sin which dwells within me.

²¹So I find it to be a law that when I want to do right, evil lies close at hand. ²²For I delight in the law of God, in my inmost self, ²³but I see in my members another law at war with the law of my mind and making me captive to the law of sin which dwells in my members. ²⁴How wretched I am! Who will deliver me from this body of death? ²⁵Thanks be to God through Jesus Christ our Sovereign![□] So then, I of myself serve the law of God with my mind, but with my flesh I serve the law of sin.

[□]RSV *king*. See Appendix.   [□]RSV *Lord*. See Appendix.

⁸:¹There is therefore now no condemnation for those who are in Christ Jesus. ²For the law of the Spirit of life in Christ Jesus has set me free from the law of sin and death. ³By sending God's own Child° in the likeness of sinful flesh, God has done what the law, weakened by the flesh, could not do. God condemned sin in the flesh ⁴in order that the just requirement of the law might be fulfilled in us, who walk not according to the flesh but according to the Spirit. ⁵For those who live according to the flesh set their minds on the things of the flesh, but those who live according to the Spirit set their minds on the things of the Spirit. ⁶To set the mind on the flesh is death, but to set the mind on the Spirit is life and peace. ⁷For the mind that is set on the flesh is hostile to God; it does not submit to God's law, indeed it cannot; ⁸and those who are in the flesh cannot please God.

⁹But you are not in the flesh, you are in the Spirit, if in fact the Spirit of God dwells in you. Any one who does not have the Spirit of Christ does not belong to Christ. ¹⁰But if Christ is in you, although your bodies are dead because of sin, your spirits are alive because of righteousness. ¹¹If the Spirit of the one who raised Jesus from the dead dwells in you, the one who raised Christ Jesus from the dead will give life to your mortal bodies also through that same Spirit which dwells in you.

¹²So then, brothers and sisters, we are debtors, not to the flesh, to live according to the flesh—¹³for if you live according to the flesh you will die, but if by the Spirit you put to death the deeds of the body you will live.

Gospel ~ Matthew 11:25-30

Jesus speaks of the relationship of the Child of God to God the Father and Mother.

²⁵At that time Jesus declared, "I thank you, [*God my Mother and**] Father, Sovereign◻ of heaven and earth, that you have hidden these things from the wise and understanding and revealed them to babes; ²⁶yea, God,⊗ for such was your gracious will. ²⁷All things have been delivered to me by [*God*] my Father [*and Mother**]; and no one knows the Child° except God,⊗ and no one knows God⊗ except the Child° and any one to whom the Child° chooses to reveal God. ²⁸Come to me, all who labor and are heavy laden, and I will give you rest. ²⁹Take my yoke upon you, and learn from me; for I am gentle and lowly in heart, and you will find rest for your souls. ³⁰For my yoke is easy, and my burden is light."

°RSV Rom. 8:1 *his own Son;* Matt. 11:27 *Son.* See Appendix.
*Addition to the text. See "Metaphor" and "God the Father and Mother" in the Appendix.
◻RSV *Lord.* See Appendix.   ⊗RSV *Father.*

PENTECOST 8

The prophet Isaiah bids everyone who is thirsty to come to God and be satisfied by the word of God.

¹Ho, every one who thirsts,
    come to the waters;
and any one who has no money,
    come, buy and eat!
Come, buy wine and milk
    without money and without price.
²Why do you spend your money for that which is not bread,
    and your labor for that which does not satisfy?
Hearken diligently to me, and eat what is good,
    and delight yourselves in fatness.
³Incline your ear, and come to me;
    hear, that your soul may live;
and I will make with you an everlasting covenant,
    my steadfast, sure love for David.
⁴Behold, I made David a witness to the peoples,
    a leader and commander for the peoples.
⁵Behold, you shall call nations that you know not,
    and nations that knew you not shall run to you,
because of the SOVEREIGN ONE your God, and of the Holy One of Israel,
    for God has glorified you. . . .
¹⁰For as the rain and the snow come down from heaven,
    and return not thither but water the earth,
making it bring forth and sprout,
    giving seed to the sower and bread to the eater,
¹¹so shall my word be that goes forth from my mouth;
    it shall not return to me empty,
but it shall accomplish that which I purpose,
    and prosper in the thing for which I sent it.
¹²For you shall go out in joy,
    and be led forth in peace;
the mountains and the hills before you
    shall break forth into singing,
    and all the trees of the field shall clap their hands.
¹³Instead of the thorn shall come up the cypress;
    instead of the brier shall come up the myrtle;
and it shall be to GOD for a memorial,
    for an everlasting sign which shall not be cut off.

The apostle Paul speaks of the groaning of the whole creation and of waiting, along with the children of God, for redemption.

[18]I consider that the sufferings of this present time are not worth comparing with the glory that is to be revealed to us. [19]For the creation waits with eager longing for the revealing of the children of God; [20]for the creation was subjected to futility, not of its own will but by the will of God who subjected it in hope; [21]because the creation itself will be set free from its bondage to decay and obtain the glorious liberty of the children of God. [22]We know that the whole creation has been groaning in travail together until now; [23]and not only the creation, but we ourselves, who have the first fruits of the Spirit, groan inwardly as we wait for adoption as the children of God, the redemption of our bodies. [24]For in this hope we were saved. Now hope that is seen is not hope. For who hopes for what is already seen? [25]But if we hope for what we do not see, we wait for it with patience.

Gospel ~ Matthew 13:1-23

Jesus tells the parable of the sower.

[1]That same day Jesus went out of the house and sat beside the sea. [2]And great crowds gathered around, so that Jesus got into a boat and sat there; and the whole crowd stood on the beach. [3]And Jesus told them many things in parables, saying: "A sower went out to sow. [4]And as the seeds were being scattered, some seeds fell along the path, and the birds came and devoured them. [5]Other seeds fell on rocky ground, where they had not much soil, and immediately they sprang up, since they had no depth of soil, [6]but when the sun rose they were scorched; and since they had no root they withered away. [7]Other seeds fell upon thorns, and the thorns grew up and choked them. [8]Other seeds fell on good soil and brought forth grain, some a hundredfold, some sixty, some thirty. [9]Those who have ears, let them hear."

[10]Then the disciples came and said to Jesus, "Why do you speak to them in parables?" [11]And Jesus answered them, "To you it has been given to know the secrets of the realm* of heaven, but to them it has not been given. [12]For to those who have will more be given, and they will have abundance; but from those who have not, even what they have will be taken away. [13]This is why I speak to them in parables, because seeing they do not see,

---

*RSV *kingdom.* See Appendix.

and hearing they do not hear, nor do they understand. [14]With them indeed is fulfilled the prophecy of Isaiah which says:

'You shall indeed hear but never understand,
  and you shall indeed see but never perceive.
[15]For this people's heart has grown dull,
  and their ears are heavy of hearing,
  and their eyes they have closed,
 lest they should perceive with their eyes,
  and hear with their ears,
 and understand with their heart,
  and turn for me to heal them.'

[16]But blessed are your eyes, for they see, and your ears, for they hear. [17]Truly, I say to you, many prophets and righteous people longed to see what you see, and did not see it, and to hear what you hear, and did not hear it.

[18]"Hear then the parable of the sower. [19]When any hear the word of the realm* of heaven and do not understand it, the evil one comes and snatches away what is sown in the heart; this is what was sown along the path. [20]As for what was sown on rocky ground, this is the one who hears the word and immediately receives it with joy; [21]yet having no root within endures for a while, and when tribulation or persecution arises on account of the word, immediately falls away. [22]As for what was sown among thorns, this is the one who hears the word, but the cares of the world and the delight in riches choke the word, and it proves unfruitful. [23]As for what was sown on good soil, this is the one who hears the word and understands it, who indeed bears fruit, and yields, in one case a hundredfold, in another sixty, and in another thirty."

---

*RSV *kingdom*. See Appendix.

PENTECOST 9

Lesson 1 ~ Isaiah 44:6-8

God, the Redeemer, proclaims: "I am the first and I am the last." No one is to be afraid.

⁶Thus says GOD, the Ruler▢ of Israel
and the Redeemer, the GOD of hosts:
"I am the first and I am the last;
besides me there is no god.
⁷Who is like me? Speak out!
Declare it and set it forth before me.
Who has announced from of old the things to come?
Let them tell us what is yet to be.
⁸Fear not, nor be afraid;
have I not told you from of old and declared it?
And you are my witnesses!
Is there a God besides me?
There is no Rock; I know not any."

Lesson 1 (alternate) ~ Wisdom of Solomon 12:13; 13:16-19

The writer reflects on the futility of prayers that are not directed to God.

¹³For neither is there any god besides you, whose care is for all people,
to whom you should prove that you have not judged unjustly. . . .
¹³:¹⁶So skilled woodcutters take thought for a carved figure, that it may not
fall,
because they know that it cannot help itself,
for it is only an image and has need of help.
¹⁷When they pray about possessions and their marriage and children,
they are not ashamed to address a lifeless thing.
¹⁸For health they appeal to a thing that is weak;
for life they pray to a thing that is dead;
for aid they entreat a thing that is utterly inexperienced;
for a prosperous journey, a thing that cannot take a step;
¹⁹for money-making and work and success with their hands
they ask strength of a thing whose hands have no strength.

▢RSV *King*. See Appendix.

Lesson 2 ~ Romans 8:26-27

Having spoken about the hope of redemption, Paul continues.

26The Spirit helps us in our weakness; for we do not know how to pray as we ought, but the Spirit itself intercedes for us with sighs too deep for words. 27And God who searches human hearts knows what is the mind of the Spirit, because the Spirit intercedes for the saints according to the will of God.

Gospel ~ Matthew 13:24-43

Jesus tells three parables.

24Jesus put a parable before them, saying, "The realm* of heaven may be compared to someone who sowed good seed in a field; 25but while everyone was sleeping, an enemy came and sowed weeds among the wheat, and went away. 26So when the plants came up and bore grain, then the weeds appeared also. 27And the servants of the householder came and asked, 'Did you not sow good seed in your field? How then has it weeds?' 28The householder said to them, 'An enemy has done this.' The servants replied, 'Then do you want us to go and gather them?' 29But the householder said, 'No; lest in gathering the weeds you root up the wheat along with them. 30Let both grow together until the harvest; and at harvest time I will tell the reapers, Gather the weeds first and bind them in bundles to be burned, but gather the wheat into my barn.' "

31Another parable Jesus put before them, saying, "The realm* of heaven is like a grain of mustard seed which someone took and sowed in a field; 32it is the smallest of all seeds, but when it has grown it is the greatest of shrubs and becomes a tree, so that the birds of the air come and make nests in its branches."

33Jesus told them another parable. "The realm* of heaven is like leaven which a woman took and hid in three measures of flour, till it was all leavened."

34All this Jesus said to the crowds in parables; indeed he said nothing to them without a parable. 35This was to fulfil what was spoken by the prophet:
"I will open my mouth in parables,
I will utter what has been hidden since the foundation of the world."

36Then Jesus left the crowds and went into the house. And the disciples

---

*RSV *kingdom*. See Appendix.

came to him, saying, "Explain to us the parable of the weeds of the field."
³⁷Jesus answered, "The one who sows the good seed is the Human One;°
³⁸the field is the world, and the good seed means the children of the
heavenly realm;* the weeds are the children of the evil one, ³⁹and the
enemy who sowed them is the devil; the harvest is the close of the age, and
the reapers are angels. ⁴⁰Just as the weeds are gathered and burned with
fire, so will it be at the close of the age. ⁴¹The Human One° will send
angels, and they will gather out of the world all causes of sin and all
evildoers, ⁴²and throw them into the furnace of fire where there shall be
weeping and gnashing of teeth. ⁴³Then the righteous will shine like the sun
in the realm* of their God.⊗ Those who have ears, let them hear."

°RSV *Son of man.* See Appendix.
*RSV v. 38 *of the kingdom;* v. 43 *kingdom.* See Appendix.
⊗RSV *Father.*

PENTECOST 10

Lesson 1 ~ 1 Kings 3:5-12

Solomon, the ruler of Israel, prays to God to be able to discern between good and evil.

⁵At Gibeon the Sᴏᴠᴇʀᴇɪɢɴ Oɴᴇ appeared to Solomon in a dream by night; and God said, "Ask what I shall give you." ⁶And Solomon said, "You have shown great and steadfast love to your servant David my father, because he walked before you in faithfulness, in righteousness, and in uprightness of heart toward you; and you have kept for David this great and steadfast love, and have given him an heir to sit on his throne this day. ⁷And now, O Sᴏᴠᴇʀᴇɪɢɴ Oɴᴇ my God, you have made your servant king in place of David my father, although I am but a little child; I do not know how to go out or come in. ⁸And your servant is in the midst of your people whom you have chosen, a great people, that cannot be numbered or counted for multitude. ⁹Give your servant therefore an understanding mind to govern your people, that I may discern between good and evil; for who is able to govern this your great people?"

¹⁰It pleased the Sᴏᴠᴇʀᴇɪɢɴ Oɴᴇ that Solomon had asked this. ¹¹And God replied, "Because you have asked this, and have not asked for yourself long life or riches or the life of your enemies, but have asked for yourself understanding to discern what is right, ¹²behold, I now do according to your word. Behold, I give you a wise and discerning mind, so that none like you has been before you and none like you shall arise after you."

Lesson 2 ~ Romans 8:28-30

The apostle Paul proclaims that God always works for the good of those who love God.

²⁸We know that in everything God works for good with those who love God, who are called according to God's purpose. ²⁹For those whom God foreknew were also predestined to be conformed to the image of God's Child,◇ in order that Christ might be the first-born among many believers. ³⁰And those whom God predestined God also called; and those whom God called God also justified; and those whom God justified God also glorified.

◇RSV *Son.* See Appendix.

Jesus speaks in three different ways about the realm of heaven.

44The realm* of heaven is like treasure hidden in a field, which someone found and covered up; then in great joy the finder goes and sells everything and buys that field.

45Again, the realm* of heaven is like a merchant in search of fine pearls, 46who, on finding one pearl of great value, went and sold everything and bought it.

47Again, the realm* of heaven is like a net which was thrown into the sea and gathered fish of every kind; 48when the net was full, it was drawn ashore and people sat down and sorted the good into vessels but threw away the bad. 49So it will be at the close of the age. The angels will come out and separate the evil from the righteous, 50and throw them into the furnace of fire, where there will be weeping and gnashing of teeth.

51"Have you understood all this?" They answered, "Yes." 52And Jesus said to them, "Therefore every scribe who has been trained for the realm* of heaven is like a householder who brings out of the treasury what is new and what is old."

---

*RSV *kingdom*. See Appendix.

PENTECOST 11

Lesson 1 ~ Nehemiah 9:16-20

Ezra proclaims publicly the sin of Israel, and the mercies of God.

[16]Our ancestors acted presumptuously and stiffened their neck and did not obey your commandments; [17]they refused to obey, and were not mindful of the wonders which you performed among them; but they stiffened their neck and appointed a leader to return to their bondage in Egypt. But you are a God ready to forgive, gracious and merciful, slow to anger and abounding in steadfast love, and did not forsake them. [18]Even when they had made for themselves a molten calf and said, "This is your God who brought you up out of Egypt," and had committed great blasphemies, [19]you in your great mercies did not forsake them in the wilderness; the pillar of cloud which led them in the way did not depart from them by day, nor the pillar of fire by night which lighted for them the way by which they should go. [20]You gave your good Spirit to instruct them, and did not withhold your manna from their mouth, and gave them water for their thirst.

Lesson 2 ~ Romans 8:31-39

In a lyrical passage Paul glories in the love of God in Christ Jesus.

[31]What then shall we say to this? If God is for us, who is against us? [32]God who did not spare God's own Child◊ but gave up that Child for us all, will not that God also give us all things with Christ Jesus? [33]Who shall bring any charge against God's elect? It is God who justifies; [34]who is to condemn? Is it Christ Jesus, who died, yes, who was raised from the dead, who is at the right hand of God, who indeed intercedes for us? [35]Who shall separate us from the love of Christ? Shall tribulation, or distress, or persecution, or famine, or nakedness, or peril, or sword? [36]As it is written,
"For your sake we are being killed all the day long;
we are regarded as sheep to be slaughtered."
[37]No, in all these things we are more than conquerors through the one who loved us. [38]For I am sure that neither death, nor life, nor angels, nor principalities, nor things present, nor things to come, nor powers, [39]nor height, nor depth, nor anything else in all creation, will be able to separate us from the love of God in Christ Jesus our Sovereign.□

◊RSV *Son.* See Appendix.
□RSV *Lord.* See Appendix.

Jesus feeds the five thousand.

[13]Jesus withdrew in a boat to a lonely place apart. But when the crowds heard it, they followed on foot from the towns. [14]And going ashore, Jesus saw a great throng and had compassion on them, and healed their sick. [15]When it was evening, the disciples returned, saying, "This is a lonely place, and the day is now over; send the crowds away to go into the villages and buy food for themselves." [16]Jesus said, "They need not go away; you give them something to eat." [17]They replied, "We have only five loaves here and two fish." [18]Jesus said, "Bring them here to me." [19]Then he ordered the crowds to sit down on the grass; and taking the five loaves and the two fish Jesus looked up to heaven, and blessed, and broke and gave the loaves to the disciples, and the disciples gave them to the crowds. [20]And they all ate and were satisfied. And they took up twelve baskets full of the broken pieces left over. [21]And those who ate were about five thousand men and women and children.

PENTECOST 12

Lesson 1 ~ 1 Kings 19:9-18

The story is told of Elijah in a cave of Mount Horeb.

⁹Elijah came to a cave, and lodged there; and behold, the word of GOD came to him, saying, "What are you doing here, Elijah?" ¹⁰He said, "I have been very jealous for the SOVEREIGN ONE, the God of hosts; for the people of Israel have forsaken your covenant, thrown down your altars, and slain your prophets with the sword; and I, even I only, am left; and they seek my life, to take it away." ¹¹The answer came, "Go forth, and stand upon the mount before GOD." And behold, GOD passed by, and a great and strong wind rent the mountains, and broke in pieces the rocks before GOD, but GOD was not in the wind; and after the wind an earthquake, but GOD was not in the earthquake; ¹²and after the earthquake a fire, but GOD was not in the fire; and after the fire a still small voice. ¹³And when Elijah heard it, he wrapped his face in his mantle and went out and stood at the entrance of the cave. And behold, there came a voice saying, "What are you doing here, Elijah?" ¹⁴He answered, "I have been very jealous for the SOVEREIGN ONE, the God of hosts; for the people of Israel have forsaken your covenant, thrown down your altars, and slain your prophets with the sword; and I, even I only, am left; and they seek my life, to take it away." ¹⁵And GOD said to Elijah, "Go, return on your way to the wilderness of Damascus; and when you arrive, you shall anoint Hazael to be king over Syria; ¹⁶and Jehu the son of Nimshi you shall anoint to be king over Israel; and Elisha the son of Shaphat of Abelmeholah you shall anoint to be prophet in your place. ¹⁷And any one who escapes from the sword of Hazael shall Jehu slay; and whoever escapes from the sword of Jehu shall Elisha slay. ¹⁸Yet I will leave seven thousand in Israel, all the knees that have not bowed to Baal, and every mouth that has not kissed Baal."

Lesson 2 ~ Romans 9:1-5

Paul speaks out of anguish for his own people.

¹I am speaking the truth in Christ, I am not lying; my conscience bears me witness in the Holy Spirit, ²that I have great sorrow and unceasing anguish in my heart. ³For I could wish that I myself were accursed and cut off from Christ for the sake of my own people, and my kinsfolk by race. ⁴They are Israelites, and to them belong the adoption as heirs, the glory, the covenants, the giving of the law, the worship, and the promises; ⁵to them belong the ancestors in faith, and of their race, according to the flesh, is the Christ. God who is over all be blessed for ever. Amen.

Jesus comes to the disciples, who are in a boat on the sea.

²²Jesus made the disciples get into the boat and go on ahead to the other side, while he dismissed the crowds. ²³After dismissing the crowds, he went up on the mountain alone to pray. When evening came, Jesus was there alone, ²⁴but the boat by this time was many furlongs distant from the land, beaten by the waves; for the wind was against them. ²⁵And in the fourth watch of the night Jesus came to the disciples, walking on the sea. ²⁶But when the disciples saw Jesus walking on the sea, they were terrified, saying, "It is a ghost!" And they cried out in fear. ²⁷But immediately Jesus spoke to them, saying, "Take heart, it is I; have no fear."

²⁸And Peter answered, "My Sovereign,□ if it is you, bid me come to you on the water." ²⁹Jesus said, "Come." So Peter got out of the boat and walked on the water and came to Jesus; ³⁰but seeing the wind, Peter was afraid and, beginning to sink, cried out, "My Sovereign,□ save me." ³¹Jesus immediately reached out and caught Peter, saying, "O you of little faith, why did you doubt?" ³²And when Jesus and Peter got into the boat, the wind ceased. ³³And those in the boat worshiped Jesus, saying, "Truly you are the Child◇ of God."

□RSV *Lord.* See Appendix.
◇RSV *Son.* See Appendix.

PENTECOST 13

Lesson 1 ~ Isaiah 56:1-8

God commands the people to be righteous and says that those who keep the law will be made joyful.

¹Thus says GOD:
  "Keep justice, and do righteousness,
 for soon my salvation will come,
  and my deliverance be revealed.
²Blessed are those who do this,
  and the ones who hold it fast,
 who keep the sabbath, not profaning it,
  and keep their hands from doing any evil."
³Let not the foreigners who have joined themselves to GOD say,
  "GOD will surely separate us from the chosen people";
 and let not the eunuch say,
  "Behold, I am a dry tree."
⁴For thus says GOD:
 "To the eunuchs who keep my sabbaths,
  who choose the things that please me
  and hold fast my covenant,
⁵I will give in my house and within my walls
  a monument and a name
  better than sons and daughters;
 I will give them an everlasting name
  which shall not be cut off.
⁶And the foreigners who join themselves to me,
  to minister to me, to love my name,
  and to be my servants,
 every one who keeps the sabbath, and does not profane it,
  and holds fast my covenant—
⁷these I will bring to my holy mountain,
  and make them joyful in my house of prayer;
 their burnt offerings and their sacrifices
  will be accepted on my altar;
 for my house shall be called a house of prayer
  for all peoples.
⁸Thus says the Sovereign GOD,
  who gathers the outcasts of Israel,
 I will gather in yet others
  besides those already gathered."

Paul speaks of his own people, the Jews, and of the irrevocable character of God's call to them.

[13]Now I am speaking to you Gentiles. Inasmuch then as I am an apostle to the Gentiles, I magnify my ministry [14]in order to make my own people jealous, and thus save some of them. [15]For if their rejection means the reconciliation of the world, what will their acceptance mean but life from the dead? [16]If the dough offered as first fruits is holy, so is the whole lump; and if the root is holy, so are the branches. . . .

[29]For the gifts and the call of God are irrevocable. [30]Just as you were once disobedient to God but now have received mercy because of their disobedience, [31]so have they now been disobedient in order that by the mercy shown to you they also may receive mercy. [32]For God has consigned all to disobedience, that God may have mercy upon all.

Gospel ~ Matthew 15:21-28

Matthew tells the story of Jesus and the Canaanite woman who comes for mercy.

[21]And Jesus went away from there and withdrew to the district of Tyre and Sidon. [22]And behold, a Canaanite woman from that region came out and cried, "Have mercy on me, O Sovereign,□ Son of David, my daughter is severely possessed by a demon." [23]But Jesus did not answer her a word. And the disciples came and begged Jesus, saying, "Send her away, for she is crying after us." [24]Jesus answered, " I was sent only to the lost sheep of the house of Israel." [25]But she came and knelt before Jesus, saying, "O Sovereign,□ help me." [26]And Jesus answered, "It is not fair to take the children's bread and throw it to the dogs." [27]She said, "Yes, my Sovereign,□ yet even the dogs eat the crumbs that fall from their owners' table." [28]Then Jesus answered her, "O woman, great is your faith! Be it done for you as you desire." And her daughter was healed instantly.

□RSV *Lord.* See Appendix.

PENTECOST 14

Lesson 1 ~ Isaiah 22:19-23

The prophet Isaiah proclaims the downfall of Shebna, the king's steward, and the promotion of Eliakim.

¹⁹I will thrust you from your office, and you will be cast down from your station. ²⁰In that day I will call my servant Eliakim the son of Hilkiah, ²¹and I will clothe Eliakim with your robe, and will bind your girdle on him, and will commit your authority to the hand of Eliakim who shall be a father to the inhabitants of Jerusalem and to the house of Judah. ²²And I will place on the shoulder of Eliakim the key of the house of David; Eliakim shall open, and none shall shut; and he shall shut, and none shall open. ²³And I will fasten Eliakim like a peg in a sure place, and he will become a throne of honor to the house of Hilkiah.

Lesson 2 ~ Romans 11:33-36

Paul writes of the mystery and the inscrutability of the ways of God.

³³O the depth of the riches and wisdom and knowledge of God! How unsearchable are God's judgments and how inscrutable God's ways!
    ³⁴"For who has known the mind of the Sovereign,□
      or who has been God's counselor?"
    ³⁵"Or who has given a gift to the Sovereign
      in order to be repaid?"
³⁶For from God and through God and to God are all things. To God be glory for ever. Amen.

Gospel ~ Matthew 16:13-20

Jesus asks the disciples who various people are saying the Human One is, and Simon Peter answers for himself.

¹³Now coming into the district of Caesarea Philippi, Jesus asked the disciples, "Who do people say that the Human One° is?" ¹⁴And they said,

---

□RSV *Lord.* See Appendix.
°RSV *Son of man.* See Appendix.

"Some say John the Baptist, others say Elijah, and others Jeremiah or one of the prophets." 15Jesus said to them, "But who do you say that I am?" 16Simon Peter replied, "You are the Christ, the Child° of the living God." 17And Jesus answered Peter, "Blessed are you, Simon Bar-Jona! For flesh and blood has not revealed this to you, but [God] my Father [and Mother*] who is in heaven. 18And I tell you, you are Peter, and on this rock I will build my church, and the powers of death shall not prevail against it. 19I will give you the keys of the realm* of heaven, and whatever you bind on earth shall be bound in heaven, and whatever you loose on earth shall be loosed in heaven." 20Then Jesus strictly charged the disciples to say to no one, "Jesus is the Christ."

°RSV *Son*. See Appendix.
*Addition to the text. See "Metaphor" and "God the Father and Mother" in the Appendix.
*RSV *kingdom*. See Appendix.

PENTECOST 15

Lesson 1 ~ Jeremiah 15:15-21

Jeremiah pleads with God and God answers him.

¹⁵O GOD, you know;
   remember me and visit me,
   and take vengeance for me on my persecutors.
 In your forbearance take me not away;
   know that for your sake I bear reproach.
¹⁶Your words were found, and I ate them,
   and your words became to me a joy
   and the delight of my heart;
 for I am called by your name,
   O SOVEREIGN ONE, God of hosts.
¹⁷I did not sit in the company of merrymakers,
   nor did I rejoice;
 I sat alone, because your hand was upon me,
   for you had filled me with indignation.
¹⁸Why is my pain unceasing,
   my wound incurable,
   refusing to be healed?
 Will you be to me like a deceitful brook,
   like waters that fail?
¹⁹Therefore thus says GOD:
 "If you return, I will restore you,
   and you shall stand before me.
 If you utter what is precious, and not what is worthless,
   you shall be as my mouth.
 They shall turn to you,
   but you shall not turn to them.
²⁰And I will make you to this people
   a fortified wall of bronze;
 they will fight against you,
   but they shall not prevail over you,
 for I am with you
   to save you and deliver you,

                                        says GOD.
²¹I will deliver you out of the hand of the wicked,
   and redeem you from the grasp of the ruthless."

Lesson 2 ~ Romans 12:1-8

Paul writes to the Roman Christians that they, with their diverse gifts, are one body in Christ.

¹I appeal to you therefore, sisters and brothers, by the mercies of God, to present your bodies as a living sacrifice, holy and acceptable to God, which is your spiritual worship. ²Do not be conformed to this world but be transformed by the renewal of your mind, that you may prove what is the will of God, what is good and acceptable and perfect.

³For by the grace given to me I bid every one among you not to think of yourself more highly than you ought to think, but to think with sober judgment, each according to the measure of faith which God has assigned you. ⁴For as in one body we have many members, and all the members do not have the same function, ⁵so we, though many, are one body in Christ, and individually members one of another. ⁶Having gifts that differ according to the grace given us, let us use them: if prophecy, in proportion to our faith; ⁷if service, in our serving; the one who teaches, in teaching; ⁸the one who exhorts, in exhortation; the one who contributes, in liberality; the one who gives aid, with zeal; the one who does acts of mercy, with cheerfulness.

Gospel ~ Matthew 16:21-28

Jesus tells the disciples about what lies ahead, and about what his future will mean for them.

²¹From that time Jesus began to show the disciples that he must go to Jerusalem and suffer many things from the elders and chief priests and scribes, and be killed, and on the third day be raised. ²²And Peter took Jesus and spoke in rebuke, "God forbid! This shall never happen to you." ²³But Jesus turned and said to Peter, "Get behind me, Satan! You are a hindrance to me; for you are not on God's side, but on the human side."

²⁴Then Jesus told the disciples, "If any would come after me, let them deny themselves and take up their cross and follow me. ²⁵For those who would save their life will lose it, and those who lose their life for my sake will find it. ²⁶For what is one profited, if one gains the whole world and forfeits one's life? Or what shall one give in return for one's life? ²⁷For the Human One° is to come with the angels in the heavenly glory of God, and will then repay every one for their actions. ²⁸Truly, I say to you, there are some standing here who will not taste death before they see the Human One° coming in power and glory."

°RSV *Son of man.* See Appendix.

PENTECOST 16

Lesson 1 ~ Ezekiel 33:1-11

The prophet Ezekiel is a watcher.

[1]The word of GOD came to me; [2]"O mortal,** speak to your people and say to them, If I bring the sword upon a land, and the people of the land take a person from among them, and make that person their watcher; [3]and if the watcher sees the sword coming upon the land and blows the trumpet and warns the people; [4]then if any who hear the sound of the trumpet do not take warning, and the sword comes and takes them away, their blood shall be upon their own heads. [5]They heard the sound of the trumpet, and did not take warning; their blood shall be upon themselves. But if they had taken warning, they would have saved their lives. [6]But if the watcher sees the sword coming and does not blow the trumpet, so that the people are not warned, and the sword comes, and takes any of them; they are taken away in their iniquity, but their blood I will require at the watcher's hand.

[7]"So you, O mortal,** I have made a watcher for the house of Israel; whenever you hear a word from my mouth, you shall give them warning from me. [8]If I say to the wicked, O wicked one, you shall surely die, and you do not speak to warn the wicked to turn from their ways, the wicked shall die in their iniquity, but their blood I will require at your hand. [9]But if you warn the wicked to turn from their wicked ways, and they do not turn from their wicked ways, they shall die in their iniquity, but you will have saved your life.

[10]"And you, O mortal,** say to the house of Israel, Thus have you said: 'Our transgressions and our sins are upon us and we waste away because of them; how then can we live?' [11]Say to them, As I live, says the Sovereign GOD, I have no pleasure in the death of the wicked, but that the wicked turn from their ways and live; turn back, turn back from your evil ways; for why will you die, O house of Israel?"

Lesson 2 ~ Romans 12:9–13:10

Paul exhorts believers and speaks about their relationships to authorities.

[9]Let love be genuine; hate what is evil, hold fast to what is good; [10]be affectionately devoted to one another, outdo one another in showing honor. [11]Never flag in zeal, be aglow with the Spirit, serve the Sovereign.□ [12]Rejoice in your hope, be patient in tribulation, be constant in prayer. [13]Contribute to the needs of the saints, practice hospitality.

[14]Bless those who persecute you; bless and do not curse them. [15]Rejoice with those who rejoice, weep with those who weep. [16]Live in harmony with one another; do not be haughty, but associate with the lowly; never be conceited. [17]Repay no one evil for evil, but take thought for what is noble in the sight of all. [18]If possible, so far as it depends upon you, live

---

** RSV v. 2 *Son of man;* vs. 7, 10 *son of man.*
□ RSV *Lord.* See Appendix.

peaceably with all. ¹⁹Beloved, never avenge yourselves but leave it to the wrath of God; for it is written, "Vengeance is mine, I will repay, says the Sovereign."□ ²⁰No, "if your enemies are hungry, feed them; if they are thirsty, give them drink; for by so doing you will heap burning coals upon their heads." ²¹Do not be overcome by evil, but overcome evil with good.

^{13:1}Let every person be subject to the governing authorities. For there is no authority except from God, and those that exist have been instituted by God. ²Therefore whoever resists the authorities resists what God has appointed, and those who resist will incur judgment. ³For rulers are not a terror to good conduct, but to bad. Would you have no fear of authority? Then do what is good, and you will receive approval, ⁴for the one in authority is God's servant for your good. But if you do wrong, be afraid, for the authority does not bear the sword in vain, but is the servant of God to execute God's wrath on the wrongdoer. ⁵Therefore one must be subject, not only to avoid God's wrath but also for the sake of conscience. ⁶For the same reason you also pay taxes, for the authorities are ministers of God, attending to this very thing. ⁷Pay all of them their dues, taxes to whom taxes are due, revenue to whom revenue is due, respect to whom respect is due, honor to whom honor is due.

⁸Owe no one anything, except to love one another; for whoever loves one's neighbor has fulfilled the law. ⁹The commandments, "You shall not commit adultery, You shall not kill, You shall not steal, You shall not covet," and any other commandment, are summed up in this sentence, "You shall love your neighbor as yourself." ¹⁰Love does no wrong to a neighbor; therefore love is the fulfilling of the law.

Gospel ~ Matthew 18:15-20

Jesus responds to a question from the disciples, stating the practice the church is to follow if our neighbor sins against us.

¹⁵If your neighbor in the church sins against you, go and point out the fault between the two of you alone. If your neighbor listens to you, you have gained your neighbor. ¹⁶But if your neighbor does not listen, take one or two others along with you, that every word may be confirmed by the evidence of two or three witnesses. ¹⁷If your neighbor refuses to listen to them, tell it to the church; and if your neighbor refuses to listen to the church, let that neighbor be to you as a Gentile and a tax collector. ¹⁸Truly, I say to you, whatever you bind on earth shall be bound in heaven, and whatever you loose on earth shall be loosed in heaven. ¹⁹Again I say to you, if two of you agree on earth about anything they ask, it will be done for them by [God] my [Mother and*] Father in heaven. ²⁰For where two or three are gathered in my name, there am I in the midst of them.

□RSV *Lord*. See Appendix.
*Addition to the text. See "Metaphor" and "God the Father and Mother" in the Appendix.

PENTECOST 17

Lesson 1 ~ Genesis 50:15-21

Joseph comforted his brothers after their father died.

¹⁵When Joseph's brothers saw that their father was dead, they said, "It may be that Joseph will hate us and pay us back for all the evil which we did to him." ¹⁶So they sent a message to Joseph, saying, "Your father gave this command before he died, ¹⁷'Say to Joseph, Forgive, I pray you, the transgression of your brothers and their sin, because they did evil to you.' And now, we pray you, forgive the transgression of the servants of the God of Jacob." Joseph wept when they spoke to him. ¹⁸The brothers also came and fell down before Joseph, and said, "Behold, we are your servants." ¹⁹But Joseph said to them, "Fear not, for am I in the place of God? ²⁰As for you, you meant evil against me; but God meant it for good, to bring it about that many people should be kept alive, as they are today. ²¹So do not fear; I will provide for you and your little ones." Thus Joseph reassured them and comforted them.

Lesson 1 (alternate) ~ Ecclesiasticus (Sirach) 27:30–28:7

Ecclesiasticus, or the Wisdom of Jesus the Son of Sirach, speaks of vengeance.

³⁰Anger and wrath, these also are abominations,
　　and the sinner will possess them.
^{28:1}Any one who takes vengeance will suffer vengeance from God,
　　who will firmly establish an avenger's sins.
²Forgive your neighbors the wrong they have done,
　　and then your sins will be pardoned when you pray.
³Does any one harbor anger against another,
　　and yet seek healing from God?
⁴Does any one not show mercy toward a fellow human being,
　　and yet pray for forgiveness?
⁵If such a person, being flesh, maintains wrath,
　　who will make expiation for that person's sins?
⁶Remember the end of your life, and cease from enmity,
　　remember destruction and death, and be true to the commandments.
⁷Remember the commandments, and do not be angry with your neighbor;
　　remember the covenant of the Most High, and overlook ignorance.

Lesson 2 ~ Romans 14:5-12

Paul admonishes the Roman Christians not to pass judgment on each other.

⁵Some people esteem one day as better than another, while others esteem all days alike. Let all be fully convinced in their own mind. ⁶Those who observe the day, observe it in honor of the Sovereign.▫ Those also who eat, eat in honor of Christ, since they give thanks to God; while those who abstain, abstain in honor of Christ and give thanks to God. ⁷None of us live to ourselves, and none of us die to ourselves. ⁸If we live, we live to Christ, and if we die, we die to Christ; so then, whether we live or whether we die, we are Christ's. ⁹For to this end, Christ died and lived again, to be Sovereign▫ both of the dead and of the living.

¹⁰Why do you pass judgment on your brother or sister? Or you, why do you despise your sister or brother? For we shall all stand before the judgment seat of God; ¹¹for it is written,

"As I live, says the Sovereign,▫ every knee shall bow to me,
and every tongue shall give praise to God."
¹²So each of us shall give account of ourselves to God.

Gospel ~ Matthew 18:21-35

Jesus compares the realm of heaven to a king who wishes to settle accounts with his servants.

²¹Then Peter came up and said to Jesus, "My Sovereign,▫ how often shall my brother or sister sin against me, and I forgive them? As many as seven times?" ²²Jesus answered, "I do not say to you seven times, but seventy times seven.

²³"Therefore the realm* of heaven may be compared to a king who wished to settle accounts with every servant in the realm. ²⁴When the king began the reckoning, one servant was brought in owing ten thousand talents; ²⁵and as that servant could not pay, the king ordered that servant to be sold, with spouse and children and all possessions, and payment to be made. ²⁶So the servant fell down and implored, 'Have patience with me, and I will pay you everything.' ²⁷And out of pity the king released that servant and forgave the debt. ²⁸But that same servant went out, and came upon a co-worker who owed the first servant a hundred denarii; and seizing the debtor by the throat said, 'Pay what you owe.' ²⁹So the co-worker fell

---

▫RSV *Lord*. See Appendix.
*RSV *kingdom*. See Appendix.

down, pleading, 'Have patience with me, and I will pay you.' ³⁰But the first servant refused and went and put the debtor in prison till the debt should be paid. ³¹When the other servants saw what had taken place, they were greatly distressed, and they went and reported to their king all that had taken place. ³²Then the king summoned the first servant and said, 'You wicked servant! I forgave you all that debt because you pleaded with me; ³³and should not you have had mercy on your co-worker, as I had mercy on you?' ³⁴And in anger the king delivered that servant to the jailers, till the debt should be paid in full. ³⁵So also my God who is in heaven⊗ will do to every one of you, if you do not forgive your sister or brother from your heart."

⊗RSV *my heavenly Father*.

PENTECOST 18

Lesson 1 ~ Isaiah 55:6-11

Isaiah issues a call to repentance and trust in God's grace.

⁶Seek GOD who may be found,
  call upon God who is near;
⁷let the wicked forsake their ways,
  and the unrighteous their thoughts;
 let them return to the SOVEREIGN ONE, who will have mercy on them,
  and to our God, who will abundantly pardon.
⁸For my thoughts are not your thoughts,
  neither are your ways my ways, says GOD.
⁹For as the heavens are higher than the earth,
  so are my ways higher than your ways
  and my thoughts than your thoughts.
¹⁰For as the rain and the snow come down from heaven,
  and return not thither but water the earth,
 making it bring forth and sprout,
  giving seed to the sower and bread to the eater,
¹¹so shall my word be that goes forth from my mouth;
  it shall not return to me empty,
 but it shall accomplish that which I purpose,
  and prosper in the thing for which I sent it.

Lesson 2 ~ Philippians 1:1-11, 19-27

*Paul gives thanks to the Philippians for their partnership in the gospel,
expressing belief that his life belongs to Christ.*

¹Paul and Timothy, servants of Christ Jesus,
 To all the saints in Christ Jesus who are at Philippi, with the bishops
and deacons:
 ²Grace to you and peace from God our Father [*and Mother**], and from
the Sovereign□ Jesus Christ.
 ³I thank my God in all my remembrance of you, ⁴always in every prayer
of mine for you all making my prayer with joy, ⁵thankful for your
partnership in the gospel from the first day until now. ⁶And I am sure that

---

*Addition to the text. See "Metaphor" and "God the Father and Mother" in the Appendix.
□RSV *Lord.* See Appendix.

the one who began a good work in you will bring it to completion at the day of Jesus Christ. [7]It is right for me to feel thus about you all, because I hold you in my heart, for you are all partakers with me of grace, both in my imprisonment and in the defense and confirmation of the gospel. [8]For God is my witness, how I yearn for you all with the affection of Christ Jesus. [9]And it is my prayer that your love may abound more and more, with knowledge and all discernment, [10]so that you may approve what is excellent, and may be pure and blameless for the day of Christ, [11]filled with the fruits of righteousness which come through Jesus Christ, to the glory and praise of God. . . .

[19]Yes, and I shall rejoice. For I know that through your prayers and the help of the Spirit of Jesus Christ this will turn out for my deliverance, [20]as it is my eager expectation and hope that I shall not be at all ashamed, but that with full courage now as always Christ will be honored in my body, whether by life or by death. [21]For to me to live is Christ, and to die is gain. [22]If it is to be life in the flesh, that means fruitful labor for me. Yet which I shall choose I cannot tell. [23]I am hard pressed between the two. My desire is to depart and be with Christ, for that is better. [24]But to remain in the flesh is more necessary on your account. [25]Convinced of this, I know that I shall remain and continue with you all, for your progress and joy in the faith, [26]so that in me you may have ample cause to glory in Christ Jesus, because of my coming to you again.

[27]Only let your manner of life be worthy of the gospel of Christ, so that whether I come and see you or am absent, I may hear of you that you stand firm in one spirit, with one mind striving side by side for the faith of the gospel.

Gospel ~ Matthew 20:1-16

Jesus tells the parable of the laborers in the vineyard.

[1]For the realm* of heaven is like a householder who went out early in the morning to hire laborers for the vineyard. [2]After agreeing with the laborers for a denarius a day, the householder sent them into the vineyard. [3]And going out about the third hour the householder saw others standing idle in the market place, [4]and said to them, "You go into the vineyard too, and whatever is right I will give you." So they went. [5]Going out again about the sixth hour and the ninth hour, the householder did the same. [6]And about the eleventh hour the householder went out and found others standing, and said to them, "Why do you stand here idle all day?" [7]They

---

*RSV *kingdom*. See Appendix.

replied, "Because no one has hired us." The householder said to them, "You go into the vineyard too." [8]And when evening came, the owner of the vineyard said to the steward, "Call the laborers and pay them their wages, beginning with the last, up to the first." [9]And when those hired about the eleventh hour came, each of them received a denarius. [10]Now when the first came, they thought they would receive more; but each of them also received a denarius. [11]And on receiving it they grumbled at the householder, [12]saying, "These last worked only one hour, and you have made them equal to us who have borne the burden of the day and the scorching heat." [13]But the householder replied to one of them, "Friend, I am doing you no wrong; did you not agree with me for a denarius? [14]Take what belongs to you, and go; I choose to give to this last as I give to you. [15]Am I not allowed to do what I choose with what belongs to me? Or do you begrudge my generosity?" [16]So the last will be first, and the first last.

PENTECOST 19

Lesson 1 ~ Ezekiel 18:1-4, 25-32

Ezekiel speaks about individual responsibility.

¹The word of GOD came to me again: ²"What do you mean by repeating this proverb concerning the land of Israel, 'The parents have eaten sour grapes, and the children's teeth are set on edge'? ³As I live, says the Sovereign GOD, this proverb shall no more be used by you in Israel. ⁴Behold, all people are mine; the parents as well as the children are mine: the one that sins shall die. . . .

²⁵"Yet you say, 'The way of God is not just.' Hear now, O house of Israel: Is my way not just? ²⁶When someone righteous turns away from righteousness and commits iniquity, that one shall die for it; for the iniquity which has been committed that one shall die. ²⁷Again, when someone wicked turns away from the wickedness that has been committed and does what is lawful and right, that one shall be saved. ²⁸Having considered and turned away from all these transgressions which have been committed, that one shall surely live and shall not die. ²⁹Yet the house of Israel says, 'The way of the Sovereign is not just.' O house of Israel, are my ways not just? Is it not your ways that are not just?

³⁰"Therefore I will judge you, O house of Israel, every one according to your ways, says the Sovereign GOD. Repent and turn from all your transgressions, lest iniquity be your ruin. ³¹Cast away from you all the transgressions which you have committed against me, and get yourselves a new heart and a new spirit! Why will you die, O house of Israel? ³²For I have no pleasure in the death of any one, says the Sovereign GOD; so turn, and live."

Lesson 2 ~ Philippians 2:1-13

Paul reflects on Christ's example of humility and obedience.

¹So if there is any encouragement in Christ, any incentive of love, any participation in the Spirit, any affection and sympathy, ²complete my joy by being of the same mind, having the same love, being in full accord and of one mind. ³Do nothing from selfishness or conceit, but in humility count others better than yourselves. ⁴Let each of you look not only to your own interests, but also to the interests of others. ⁵Have this mind among yourselves, which is yours in Christ Jesus, ⁶who, though being in the form of God, did not count equality with God a thing to be grasped, ⁷but emptied self, taking the form of a servant, being born in the likeness of human

beings. [8]And being found in human form, Christ humbled self and became obedient unto death, even death on a cross. [9]Therefore God has highly exalted Jesus and bestowed on Jesus the name which is above every name, [10]that at the name of Jesus every knee should bow, in heaven and on earth and under the earth, [11]and every tongue confess that Jesus Christ is Sovereign,□ to the glory of God the Father [and Mother*].

[12]Therefore, my beloved, as you have always obeyed, so now, not only as in my presence but much more in my absence, work out your own salvation with fear and trembling; [13]for God is at work in you, both to will and to work for God's good pleasure.

Gospel ~ Matthew 21:28-32

Having spoken to the disciples about the source of his authority, Jesus told them another parable.

[28]"What do you think? Someone who owned a vineyard had two sons, and went to the first and said, 'My son, go and work in the vineyard today.' [29]And the son answered, 'I will not'; but afterward the son repented and went. [30]And the owner of the vineyard went to the second and said the same; and the second son answered, 'I go,' but did not go. [31]Which of the two did the will of the parent?" They said, "The first." Jesus said to them, "Truly, I say to you, the tax collectors and the harlots go into the realm* of God before you. [32]For John came to you in the way of righteousness, and you did not believe John, but the tax collectors and the harlots did believe him; and even when you saw it, you did not afterward repent and believe John."

□RSV *Lord.* See Appendix.
*Addition to the text. See "Metaphor" and "God the Father and Mother" in the Appendix.
✶RSV *kingdom.* See Appendix.

PENTECOST 20

An allegory of a vineyard told by Isaiah.

¹Let me sing for my beloved
   a love song concerning a vineyard:
 My beloved had a vineyard
   on a very fertile hill.
²My beloved digged it and cleared it of stones,
   and planted it with choice vines.
 My beloved built a watchtower in the midst of it,
   and hewed out a wine vat in it;
 and looked for it to yield grapes,
   but it yielded wild grapes.
³And now, O inhabitants of Jerusalem
   and people of Judah,
 judge, I pray you, between me
   and my vineyard.
⁴What more was there to do for my vineyard
   that I have not done in it?
 When I looked for it to yield grapes,
   why did it yield wild grapes?
⁵And now I will tell you
   what I will do to my vineyard.
 I will remove its hedge,
   and it shall be devoured;
 I will break down its wall,
   and it shall be trampled down.
⁶I will make it a waste;
   it shall not be pruned or hoed,
   and briers and thorns shall grow up;
 I will also command the clouds
   that they rain no rain upon it.
⁷For the vineyard of the GOD of hosts
   is the house of Israel,
 and the people of Judah
   are God's pleasant planting;
 and God looked for justice,
   but behold, bloodshed;
 for righteousness,
   but behold, a cry!

Lesson 2 ~ Philippians 3:12-21

Paul, taken hold of by Christ Jesus, exhorts his friends at Philippi.

[12]Not that I have already obtained this or am already perfect; but I press on to make it my own, because I have been taken hold of by Christ Jesus. [13]My dear sisters and brothers, I do not consider that I have made it my own; but one thing I do, forgetting what lies behind and straining forward to what lies ahead, [14]I press on toward the goal for the prize of the upward call of God in Christ Jesus. [15]Let those of us who are mature be thus minded; and if in anything you are otherwise minded, God will reveal that also to you. [16]Only let us hold true to what we have attained.

[17]Brothers and sisters, join in imitating me, and mark those who so live as you have an example in us. [18]For many, of whom I have often told you and now tell you even with tears, live as enemies of the cross of Christ. [19]Their end is destruction, their god is the belly, and they glory in their shame, with minds set on earthly things. [20]But our commonwealth is in heaven, and from it we await a Savior, the Sovereign□ Jesus Christ, [21]who will change our lowly body to be like Christ's glorious body, by the power which enables Christ even to subject all things to Christ's self.

Gospel ~ Matthew 21:33-43

Hear a parable of the realm of God.

[33]"There was a householder who planted a vineyard, and set a hedge around it, and dug a wine press in it, and built a tower, and let it out to tenants, and went into another country. [34]When the season of fruit drew near, the householder sent servants to the tenants, to get the fruit; [35]and the tenants took the servants and beat one, killed another, and stoned another. [36]Again the householder sent other servants, more than the first; and they did the same to them. [37]Afterward the householder sent the heir◇ to them, the one who would inherit the vineyard, saying, 'They will respect my heir,◇ my very own child.' [38]But when the tenants saw the owner's child,◇ they said to themselves, 'This is the heir; come, let us kill this one too and have the inheritance.' [39]And they took and cast the heir out of the vineyard, and killed the heir. [40]When therefore the owner of the vineyard comes, what will be done to those tenants?" [41]Those hearing the parable said to Jesus, "The owner will put those wretches to a miserable death, and

---

□RSV *Lord*. See Appendix.
◇RSV *son*.

let out the vineyard to other tenants who will give the owner the fruits in their seasons."

⁴²Jesus said to them, "Have you never read in the scriptures:
'The very stone which the builders rejected
has become the head of the corner;
this was the Sovereign's□ doing,
and it is marvelous in our eyes'?
⁴³Therefore I tell you, the realm* of God will be taken away from you and given to a nation producing the fruits of it."

□RSV *Lord's.* See Appendix.
*RSV *kingdom.* See Appendix.

PENTECOST 21

Lesson 1 ~ Isaiah 25:1-10a

Hear the words of thanksgiving from the prophet Isaiah.

¹O GOD, you are my God;
    I will exalt you, I will praise your name;
  for you have done wonderful things,
    plans formed of old, faithful and sure.
²For you have made the city a heap,
    the fortified city a ruin;
  the palace of aliens is a city no more,
    it will never be rebuilt.
³Therefore strong peoples will glorify you;
    cities of ruthless nations will fear you.
⁴For you have been a stronghold to the poor,
    a stronghold to the needy in distress,
    a shelter from the storm and a shade from the heat;
  for the blast of the ruthless is like a storm against a wall,
⁵ like heat in a dry place.
  You subdue the noise of the aliens;
    as heat by the shade of a cloud,
    so the song of the ruthless is stilled.

⁶On this mountain the GOD of hosts will make for all peoples a feast of fat things, a feast of wine on the lees, of fat things full of marrow, of wine on the lees well refined. ⁷And God will destroy on this mountain the covering that is cast over all peoples, the veil that is spread over all nations. ⁸God will swallow up death for ever, and the Sovereign GOD will wipe away tears from all faces, and the reproach of God's people will be taken away from all the earth; for GOD has spoken.

⁹It will be said on that day, "This is our God; the one for whom we have waited, that we might be saved. This is the SOVEREIGN ONE, for whom we have waited; let us be glad and rejoice in God's salvation."

¹⁰For the hand of GOD will rest on this mountain.

Paul gives thanks to the sisters and brothers in Philippi for their kindness to him.

⁴Rejoice in the Sovereign□ always; again I will say, Rejoice. ⁵Let every one know your forbearance. The Sovereign□ is at hand. ⁶Have no anxiety about anything, but in everything by prayer and supplication with thanksgiving let your requests be made known to God. ⁷And the peace of God, which passes all understanding, will keep your hearts and your minds in Christ Jesus.

⁸Finally, my friends, whatever is true, whatever is honorable, whatever is just, whatever is pure, whatever is lovely, whatever is gracious, if there is any excellence, if there is anything worthy of praise, think about these things. ⁹What you have learned and received and heard and seen in me, do; and the God of peace will be with you.

¹⁰I rejoice in the Sovereign□ greatly that now at length you have revived your concern for me; you were indeed concerned for me, but had no opportunity. ¹¹Not that I complain of want; for I have learned, in whatever state I am, to be content. ¹²I know how to be abased, and I know how to abound; in any and all circumstances I have learned the secret of facing plenty and hunger, abundance and want. ¹³I can do all things in Christ who strengthens me.

¹⁴Yet it was kind of you to share my trouble. ¹⁵And you Philippians yourselves know that in the beginning of the gospel, when I left Macedonia, no church entered into partnership with me in giving and receiving except you only; ¹⁶for even in Thessalonica you sent me help once and again. ¹⁷Not that I seek the gift; but I seek the fruit which increases to your credit. ¹⁸I have received full payment, and more; I am filled, having received from Epaphroditus the gifts you sent, a fragrant offering, a sacrifice acceptable and pleasing to God. ¹⁹And my God will supply every need of yours according to God's riches in glory in Christ Jesus. ²⁰To God our [*Mother and**] Father be glory for ever and ever. Amen.

□RSV *Lord*. See Appendix.

*Addition to the text. RSV *our God and Father*. See "Metaphor" and "God the Father and Mother" in the Appendix.

Jesus tells the parable of the marriage feast.

¹And again Jesus spoke to them in parables, saying, ²"The realm* of heaven may be compared to a king who gave a marriage feast for his son, ³and sent servants to call those who were invited to the marriage feast; but they would not come. ⁴Again the king sent other servants, saying, 'Tell those who are invited, Behold, I have made ready my dinner, my oxen and my fat calves are killed, and everything is ready; come to the marriage feast.' ⁵But those who were invited made light of it and went off, one to a farm, another to a business, ⁶while the rest seized the king's servants, treated them shamefully, and killed them. ⁷The king was angry, and sent his troops and destroyed those murderers and burned their city. ⁸Then the king said to the servants, 'The wedding is ready, but those invited were not worthy. ⁹Go therefore to the thoroughfares, and invite to the marriage feast as many as you find.' ¹⁰And those servants went out into the streets and gathered all whom they found, both bad and good; so the wedding hall was filled with guests.

¹¹"But when the king came in to look at the guests, he saw someone who had no wedding garment; ¹²and the king said, 'Friend, how did you get in here without a wedding garment?' And the guest was speechless. ¹³Then the king said to the attendants, 'Let the guest be bound hand and foot and cast into the night, where there will be weeping and gnashing of teeth.' ¹⁴For many are called, but few are chosen."

---

*RSV *kingdom*. See Appendix.

PENTECOST 22

Lesson 1 ~ Isaiah 45:1-7

God speaks to Cyrus, God's anointed, through the prophet Isaiah.

¹Thus says GOD to Cyrus, God's anointed,
  whose right hand I have grasped,
to subdue nations before him
  and ungird the loins of rulers,□
to open doors before him
  that gates may not be closed:
²"I will go before you
  and level the mountains,
I will break in pieces the doors of bronze
  and cut asunder the bars of iron,
³I will give you the treasures of gloom
  and the hoards in secret places,
that you may know that it is I, the SOVEREIGN ONE,
  the God of Israel, who call you by your name.
⁴For the sake of my servant Jacob,
  and Israel my chosen,
I call you by your name,
  I surname you, though you do not know me.
⁵I am GOD, and there is no other,
  besides me there is no God;
  I gird you, though you do not know me,
⁶that all may know, from the rising of the sun
  and from the west, that there is none besides me;
  I am GOD, and there is no other.
⁷I form light and create gloom,
  I make weal and create woe,
  I am GOD, who do all these things.

□RSV *kings*. See Appendix.

Lesson 2 ~ 1 Thessalonians 1:1-5a

Paul writes to the church at Thessalonica.

¹Paul, Silvanus, and Timothy,
To the church of the Thessalonians in God the [*Mother and**] Father
and in the Sovereign□ Jesus Christ:
Grace to you and peace.
²We give thanks to God always for you all, constantly mentioning you
in our prayers, ³remembering before God our Father [*and Mother**] your
work of faith and labor of love and steadfastness of hope in our Sovereign□
Jesus Christ. ⁴For we know, dear friends beloved by God, that God has
chosen you; ⁵for our gospel came to you not only in word, but also in power
and in the Holy Spirit and with full conviction.

Gospel ~ Matthew 22:15-22

Jesus responds to the Pharisees' question about paying taxes to Caesar.

¹⁵Then the Pharisees went and took counsel how to entangle Jesus in his
talk. ¹⁶And they sent their disciples to Jesus, along with the Herodians,
saying, "Teacher, we know that you are true, and teach the way of God
truthfully, and court no one's favor; for you do not regard a person's status.
¹⁷Tell us, then, what you think. Is it lawful to pay taxes to Caesar, or not?"
¹⁸But Jesus, aware of their malice, said, "Why put me to the test, you
hypocrites? ¹⁹Show me the money for the tax." And they brought him a
coin. ²⁰And Jesus said to them, "Whose likeness and inscription is this?"
²¹They said, "Caesar's." Then Jesus said to them, "Render therefore to
Caesar the things that are Caesar's, and to God the things that are God's."
²²When they heard it, they marveled; and they left him and went away.

---

*Addition to the text. RSV v. 1 *God the Father;* v. 3 *our God and Father.* See "Metaphor" and
"God the Father and Mother" in the Appendix.
□RSV *Lord.* See Appendix.

PENTECOST 23

Lesson 1 ~ Exodus 22:21-27

The God of Israel protects the legally defenseless—the sojourner and the poor.

²¹You shall not wrong or oppress a sojourner, for you were sojourners in the land of Egypt. ²²You shall not afflict any widow or orphan. ²³If you do afflict them, and they cry out to me, I will surely hear their cry; ²⁴and my wrath will burn, and I will kill you with the sword, and your wives shall become widows, and your children fatherless.

²⁵If you lend money to any of my people with you who are poor, you shall not be to them as a creditor, and you shall not exact interest from them. ²⁶If ever you take your neighbor's garment in pledge, you shall restore it before the sun goes down; ²⁷for that is your neighbor's only covering, it is a mantle for the body; in what else shall your neighbor sleep? And if any one who is poor cries to me, I will hear, for I am compassionate.

Lesson 2 ~ 1 Thessalonians 1:5b–2:8

Paul praises the Thessalonians for their faith.

⁵You know what kind of people we proved to be among you for your sake. ⁶And you became imitators of us and of the Sovereign,□ for you received the word in much affliction, with joy inspired by the Holy Spirit; ⁷so that you became an example to all the believers in Macedonia and in Achaia. ⁸For not only has the word of the Sovereign□ sounded forth from you in Macedonia and Achaia, but your faith in God has gone forth everywhere, so that we need not say anything. ⁹For they themselves report concerning us what a welcome we had among you, and how you turned to God from idols, to serve a living and true God, ¹⁰and to wait for the Child◇ from heaven, whom God raised from the dead, Jesus who delivers us from the wrath to come.

²:¹For you yourselves know, my friends, that our visit to you was not in vain; ²but though we had already suffered and been shamefully treated at Philippi, as you know, we had courage in our God to declare to you the gospel of God in the face of great opposition. ³For our appeal does not spring from error or uncleanness, nor is it made with guile; ⁴but just as we

---

□RSV *Lord.* See Appendix.
◇RSV *Son.* See Appendix.

have been approved by God to be entrusted with the gospel, so we speak, not to please human beings, but to please God who tests our hearts. [5]For we never used either words of flattery, as you know, or a cloak for greed, as God is witness; [6]nor did we seek glory from any one, whether from you or from others, though we might have made demands as apostles of Christ. [7]But we were gentle among you, like a nurse taking care of children. [8]So, being affectionately desirous of you, we were ready to share with you not only the gospel of God but also our own selves, because you had become very dear to us.

Gospel ~ Matthew 22:34-46

Jesus answers the lawyer, stating the two great commandments.

[34]But when the Pharisees heard that Jesus had silenced the Sadducees, they came together. [35]And one of them, a lawyer, asked Jesus a question, as a test. [36]"Teacher, which is the great commandment in the law?" [37]And Jesus said to him, "You shall love the Sovereign□ your God with all your heart, and with all your soul, and with all your mind. [38]This is the great and first commandment. [39]And a second is like it, You shall love your neighbor as yourself. [40]On these two commandments depend all the law and the prophets."

[41]Now while the Pharisees were gathered together, Jesus asked them a question, [42]saying, "What do you think of the Christ? Whose offspring is the Christ?" They said to Jesus, "The offspring of David." [43]Jesus said to them, "How is it then that David, inspired by the Spirit, calls the Christ Sovereign,□ saying,

[44]'God said to my Sovereign,□

Sit at my right hand,

till I put your enemies under your feet?'

[45]If David thus calls the Christ Sovereign,□ how is the Christ David's offspring?" [46]And no one was able to answer Jesus a word, nor from that day did any one dare to ask Jesus any more questions.

□RSV *Lord*. See Appendix.

PENTECOST 24

Lesson 1 ~ Malachi 1:4b–2:10

The oracle of God to Israel delivered by Malachi.

⁴"Edom may build, but I will tear down, till Edom is called the wicked country, the people with whom GOD is angry for ever." ⁵Your own eyes shall see this, and you shall say, "Great is GOD, beyond the border of Israel!"

⁶Children honor their parents, and servants those whom they serve. If then I am a parent, where is my honor? And if I am served, where is my respect? says the GOD of hosts to you, O priests, who despise my name. You say, "How have we despised your name?" ⁷By offering polluted food upon my altar. And you say, "How have we polluted it?" By thinking that GOD's table may be despised. ⁸When you offer blind animals in sacrifice, is that no evil? And when you offer those that are lame or sick, is that no evil? Present that to your governor; will the governor be pleased with you or show you favor? says the GOD of hosts. ⁹And now entreat the favor of God, that God may be gracious to us. With such a gift from your hand, will God show favor to any of you? says the GOD of hosts. ¹⁰Oh, that there were one among you who would shut the doors, that you might not kindle fire upon my altar in vain! I have no pleasure in you, says the GOD of hosts, and I will not accept an offering from your hand. ¹¹For from the rising of the sun to its setting my name is great among the nations, and in every place incense is offered to my name, and a pure offering; for my name is great among the nations, says the GOD of hosts. ¹²But you profane it when you say that GOD's table is polluted, and the food for it may be despised. ¹³"What a weariness this is," you say, and you sniff at me, says the GOD of hosts. You bring what has been taken by violence or is lame or sick, and this you bring as your offering! Shall I accept that from your hand? says GOD. ¹⁴Cursed be the cheat who has an unblemished animal in the flock, and vows it, and yet sacrifices to the Sovereign what is blemished; for I am a great Ruler,▫ says the GOD of hosts, and my name is feared among the nations.

2:1And now, O priests, this command is for you. ²If you will not listen, if you will not lay it to heart to give glory to my name, says the GOD of hosts, then I will send the curse upon you and I will curse your blessings; indeed I have already cursed them, because you do not lay it to heart. ³Behold, I will rebuke your offspring, and spread dung upon your faces, the dung of your offerings, and I will put you out of my presence. ⁴So shall you know that I have sent this command to you, that my covenant with Levi may hold, says

---

▫RSV *King.* See Appendix.

the God of hosts. [5]My covenant with Levi was a covenant of life and peace, and I gave that covenant to Levi, that he might fear; and Levi feared me, and stood in awe of my name. [6]True instruction was in his mouth, and no wrong was found on his lips. Levi walked with me in peace and uprightness, and turned many from iniquity. [7]For the lips of a priest should guard knowledge, and people should seek instruction from the mouth of the priest, for the priest is the messenger of the God of hosts. [8]But you have turned aside from the way; you have caused many to stumble by your instruction; you have corrupted the covenant of Levi, says the God of hosts, [9]and so I make you despised and abased before all the people, inasmuch as you have not kept my ways but have shown partiality in your instruction.

[10]Are we not all children of one God? Has not one God created us? Why then are we faithless to one another, profaning the covenant of our ancestors?

Lesson 2 ~ 1 Thessalonians 2:7-13, 17-20

Paul reminds the church that he worked at a trade so as not to be a burden while among them.

[7]But we were gentle among you, like a nurse taking care of children. [8]So, being affectionately desirous of you, we were ready to share with you not only the gospel of God but also our own selves, because you had become very dear to us.

[9]For you remember our labor and toil, my friends; we worked night and day, that we might not burden any of you, while we preached to you the gospel of God. [10]You are witnesses and God also, how holy and righteous and blameless was our behavior to you believers; [11]for you know how, like a parent with a child, we exhorted each one of you and encouraged you and charged you [12]to lead a life worthy of God, who calls you into God's own realm* and glory.

[13]And we also thank God constantly for this, that when you received the word of God which you heard from us, you accepted it not as a human word but as what it really is, the word of God, which is at work in you believers. . . .

[17]Brothers and sisters, since for a short time we were bereft of you, in person not in heart, we endeavored the more eagerly and with great desire to see you face to face; [18]because we wanted to come to you—I, Paul, again and again—but Satan hindered us. [19]For what is our hope or joy or crown of boasting before our Sovereign□ Jesus at the expected return? Is it not you? [20]For you are our glory and joy.

---

*RSV *kingdom.* See Appendix.
□RSV *Lord.* See Appendix.

Jesus talks to the disciples about who their true teacher is.

[1]Then Jesus said to the crowds and to his disciples, [2]"The scribes and the Pharisees sit on Moses' seat; [3]so practice and observe whatever they tell you, but not what they do; for they preach, but do not practice. [4]They bind heavy burdens, hard to bear, and lay them on people's shoulders; but they themselves will not move them with their finger. [5]They do all their deeds to be seen by others; for they make their phylacteries broad and their fringes long, [6]and they love the place of honor at feasts and the best seats in the synagogues, [7]and salutations in the market places, and being called rabbi by everyone. [8]But you are not to be called rabbi, for you have one teacher, and you are all brothers and sisters. [9]And call no teacher on earth by the title 'father,' for you have only one teacher who deserves such a title, God⊗ who is in heaven. [10]Neither be called teachers, for you have one teacher, the Christ. [11]The one who is greatest among you shall be your servant; [12]all who exalt themselves will be humbled, and all who humble themselves will be exalted."

⊗RSV *you have one Father.*

PENTECOST 26

Lesson 1 ~ Amos 5:18-24

The day of God will be a day of judgment.

¹⁸Woe to you who desire the day of GOD!
    Why would you have the day of GOD?
 It is deepest shadow, and not light;
¹⁹   as if one fled from a lion,
    and was met by a bear;
 and went into the house and leaned a hand against the wall,
    and was bitten by a serpent.
²⁰Is not the day of GOD deepest shadow, and not light,
    and gloom with no brightness in it?
²¹"I hate, I despise your feasts,
    and I take no delight in your solemn assemblies.
²²Even though you offer me your burnt offerings and cereal offerings,
    I will not accept them,
 and the peace offerings of your fatted beasts
    I will not look upon.
²³Take away from me the noise of your songs;
    to the melody of your harps I will not listen.
²⁴But let justice roll down like waters,
    and righteousness like an ever-flowing stream."

Lesson 1 (alternate) ~ Wisdom of Solomon 6:12-16

Wisdom seeks out those who desire to know her and gives them understanding.

¹²Wisdom is radiant and unfading.
 easily discerned by those who love her
 and found by those who seek her.
¹³Wisdom hastens to make herself known to those who desire her.
¹⁴The one who rises early to seek wisdom will have no difficulty,
    and will find wisdom sitting at the gates.
¹⁵To fix one's thought on wisdom is perfect understanding,
    and the one who is vigilant on account of wisdom will soon be free from
        care,
¹⁶because wisdom goes about seeking those worthy of her,
    graciously appears to them in their paths,
    and meets them in every thought.

Lesson 2 ~ 1 Thessalonians 4:13-18

Paul believes that at Christ's coming the dead will be raised first and then those who are alive.

¹³But we would not have you ignorant, sisters and brothers, concerning those who are asleep, that you may not grieve as others do who have no hope. ¹⁴For since we believe that Jesus died and rose again, even so, through Jesus, God will bring with Jesus those who have fallen asleep. ¹⁵For this we declare to you by the word of the Sovereign,□ that we who are alive, who are left until the coming of the Sovereign,□ shall not precede those who have fallen asleep. ¹⁶For the Sovereign□ will indeed descend from heaven with a cry of command, with the archangel's call, and with the sound of the trumpet of God. And the dead in Christ will rise first; ¹⁷then we who are alive, who are left, shall be caught up together with them in the clouds to meet the Sovereign□ in the air; and so we shall always be with the Sovereign.□ ¹⁸Therefore comfort one another with these words.

Gospel ~ Matthew 25:1-13

Jesus, sitting on the Mount of Olives, tells the parable of the wise and foolish maidens.

¹Then the realm* of heaven shall be compared to ten maidens who took their lamps and went to meet the bridegroom. ²Five of them were foolish, and five were wise. ³For when the foolish took their lamps, they took no oil with them; ⁴but the wise took flasks of oil with their lamps. ⁵As the bridegroom was delayed, they all slumbered and slept. ⁶But at midnight there was a cry, "Behold, the bridegroom! Come out to meet him." ⁷Then all those maidens rose and trimmed their lamps. ⁸And the foolish said to the wise, "Give us some of your oil, for our lamps are going out." ⁹But the wise replied, "Perhaps there will not be enough for us and for you; go rather to the dealers and buy for yourselves." ¹⁰And while they went to buy, the bridegroom came, and those who were ready went in with him to the marriage feast; and the door was shut. ¹¹Afterward the other maidens came also, saying, "My sovereign, my sovereign,□ open to us." ¹²But the bridegroom replied, "Truly, I say to you, I do not know you." ¹³Watch therefore, for you know neither the day nor the hour.

□RSV vs. 15, 16 *Lord;* v. 11 *Lord, lord.* See Appendix.
*RSV *kingdom.* See Appendix.

PENTECOST 27

Lesson 1 ~ Proverbs 31:10-13, 19-20, 30-31

A good wife has a status of honor, according to the author of Proverbs.

¹⁰A good wife who can find?
    She is far more precious than jewels.
¹¹The heart of her husband trusts in her,
    and he will have no lack of gain.
¹²She does him good, and not harm,
    all the days of her life.
¹³She seeks wool and flax,
    and works with willing hands. . . .
¹⁹She puts her hands to the distaff,
    and her hands hold the spindle.
²⁰She opens her hand to the poor,
    and reaches out her hands to the needy. . . .
³⁰Charm is deceitful, and beauty is vain,
    but a woman who fears GOD is to be praised.
³¹Give her of the fruit of her hands,
    and let her works praise her in the gates.

Lesson 1 (alternate) ~ Zephaniah 1:7, 12-18

Zephaniah proclaims that the day of God will be deepest shadows and not light, for Israel as well as the Gentiles.

⁷Be silent before the Sovereign GOD!
    For the day of GOD is at hand;
GOD has prepared a sacrifice
    and consecrated the guests at the sacrifice. . . .
¹²At that time I will search Jerusalem with lamps,
    and I will punish the people
who are stupefied with wine,
    those who say in their hearts,
"GOD will not do good,
    nor will GOD do ill."
¹³Their goods shall be plundered,
    and their houses laid waste.
Though they build houses,
    they shall not inhabit them;
though they plant vineyards,
    they shall not drink wine from them.

¹⁴The great day of GOD is near,
  near and hastening fast;
the sound of the day of GOD is bitter,
  the mighty warrior cries aloud there.
¹⁵A day of wrath is that day,
  a day of distress and anguish,
a day of ruin and devastation,
  a day of shadow and gloom,
a day of clouds and deepest shadows,
¹⁶ a day of trumpet blast and battle cry
against the fortified cities
  and against the lofty battlements.
¹⁷I will bring distress on the people,
  so that they shall walk like the blind,
  because they have sinned against GOD;
their blood shall be poured out like dust,
  and their flesh like dung.
¹⁸Neither their silver nor their gold
  shall be able to deliver them
  on the day of the wrath of God.
In the fire of God's jealous wrath,
  all the earth shall be consumed;
for a full, yea, sudden end
  God will make of all the inhabitants of the earth.

Lesson 2 ~ 1 Thessalonians 5:1-11

Paul expresses belief that we are children of the light and of the day and will obtain salvation through Jesus Christ.

¹But as to the times and seasons, brothers and sisters, you have no need to have anything written to you. ²For you yourselves know well that the day of the Sovereign□ will come like a thief in the night. ³When people say, "There is peace and security," then sudden destruction will come upon them as travail comes upon a woman with child, and there will be no escape. ⁴But you are not in the night, sisters and brothers, for that day to surprise you like a thief. ⁵For you are all children of light and children of the day; we are not of the night. ⁶So then let us not sleep, as others do, but let us keep awake and be sober. ⁷For those who sleep, sleep at night, and those who get drunk are drunk at night. ⁸But, since we belong to the day, let us be sober, and put on the breastplate of faith and love, and for a helmet the

---

□RSV *Lord.* See Appendix.

hope of salvation. [9]For God has not destined us for wrath, but to obtain salvation through our Sovereign□ Jesus Christ, [10]who died for us so that whether we wake or sleep we might live with Christ. [11]Therefore encourage one another and build one another up, just as you are doing.

Gospel ~ Matthew 25:14-30

Jesus tells the parable of the talents.

[14]For it will be as when someone going on a journey called in servants and entrusted to them some money, [15]giving to one five talents, to another two, to another one, to each according to their ability, and then went away. [16]The servant who had received five talents went at once and traded with the money, and made five talents more. [17]So also, the one who had the two talents made two talents more. [18]But the one who had received the one talent went and dug in the ground and hid the money. [19]Now after a long time the one who had gone away returned and settled accounts with the servants. [20]And the servant who had received the five talents came forward, bringing five talents more, saying, "Sovereign,□ you delivered to me five talents; here I have made five talents more." [21]The sovereign□ said, "Well done, good and faithful servant; you have been faithful over a little, I will set you over much; enter into the joy of your sovereign."□ [22]And the one also who had the two talents came forward, saying, "Sovereign,□ you delivered to me two talents; here I have made two talents more." [23]The reply came, "Well done, good and faithful servant; you have been faithful over a little, I will set you over much; enter into the joy of your sovereign."□ [24]The one who had received the one talent came forward, saying, "Sovereign,□ I knew you to be a demanding person, reaping where you did not sow, and gathering where you did not winnow; [25]so I was afraid, and I went and hid your talent in the ground. Here you have what is yours." [26]But the sovereign□ answered, "You wicked and slothful servant! You knew that I reap where I have not sowed, and gather where I have not winnowed? [27]Then you ought to have invested my money with the bankers, and at my coming I should have received what was my own with interest. [28]So take back the talent, and give it to the one who has the ten talents. [29]For to every one who has will more be given, and they will have abundance; but from every one who has not, even what they have will be taken away. [30]And cast the worthless servant into the outer regions, where there will be weeping and gnashing of teeth."

□RSV v. 9 *Lord;* vs. 20, 22, 24 *Master;* vs. 21, 23, 26 *master.* See "Sovereign" in the Appendix.

LAST SUNDAY AFTER PENTECOST

Lesson 1 ~ Ezekiel 34:11-17, 23-24

God is the Good Shepherd who will gather the dispersed and injured flock, and place God's servant, one like David, over the people.

[11]For thus says the Sovereign GOD: Behold, I, I myself will search for my sheep, and will seek them out. [12]As a shepherd seeks out the flock when some of the sheep have been scattered abroad, so will I seek out my sheep; and I will rescue them from all places where they have been scattered on a day of clouds and deepest shadows. [13]And I will bring them out from the peoples, and gather them from the countries, and will bring them into their own land; and I will feed them on the mountains of Israel, by the fountains, and in all the inhabited places of the country. [14]I will feed them with good pasture, and upon the mountain heights of Israel shall be their pasture; there they shall lie down in good grazing land, and on fat pasture they shall feed on the mountains of Israel. [15]I myself will be the shepherd of my sheep, and I will make them lie down, says the Sovereign GOD. [16]I will seek the lost, and I will bring back the strayed, and I will bind up the crippled, and I will strengthen the weak, and the fat and the strong I will watch over; I will feed them in justice.

[17]As for you, my flock, thus says the Sovereign GOD: Behold, I judge between sheep and sheep. . . .

[23]And I will set up over them one shepherd, my servant David, who shall feed them: David shall feed them and be their shepherd. [24]And I, the Sovereign ONE, will be their God, and my servant David shall be prince among them; I, the Sovereign GOD, have spoken.

Lesson 2 ~ 1 Corinthians 15:20-28

Paul writes of the resurrection of Christ and the subjection of all things to Christ.

[20]But in fact Christ has been raised from the dead, the first fruits of those who have fallen asleep. [21]For as by a human being came death, by a human being has come also the resurrection of the dead. [22]For as in Adam all die, so also in Christ shall all be made alive. [23]But each in the proper order: Christ the first fruits, then at Christ's coming those who belong to Christ. [24]Then comes the end, when Christ delivers all sovereignty to God the Father [*and Mother**], after Christ has destroyed every rule and every authority and every power. [25]For Christ must reign until all enemies are

---

*Addition to the text. RSV *Most High*. See "Metaphor" and "God the Father and Mother" in the Appendix.

put under Christ's feet. 26The last enemy to be destroyed is death. 27For it is written, "God has put all things in subjection under Christ's feet." But when it says, "All things are put in subjection," it is clear that God, who put all things under Christ, is not included. 28When all things are subjected to Christ, then Christ also will be subjected to God who put all things under Christ, that God may be everything to every one.

Gospel ~ Matthew 25:31-46

Jesus tells the parable of the great judgment.

31When the Human One° comes in glory, with all the angels, then that one will sit on a glorious throne. 32All the nations will be gathered before the Human One,° who will separate them one from another as a shepherd separates the sheep from the goats, 33placing the sheep on the right, but the goats on the left. 34Then the Monarch▢ will say to those on the right, "Come, O blessed of [God] my Father [*and Mother**], inherit the realm* prepared for you from the foundation of the world; 35for I was hungry and you gave me food, I was thirsty and you gave me drink, I was a stranger and you welcomed me, 36I was naked and you clothed me, I was sick and you visited me, I was in prison and you came to me." 37Then the righteous will answer, "O Sovereign,▢ when did we see you hungry and feed you, or thirsty and give you drink? 38And when did we see you a stranger and welcome you, or naked and clothe you? 39And when did we see you sick or in prison and visit you?" 40And the Monarch▢ will answer them, "Truly, I say to you, as you did it to one of the least of these my sisters and brothers, you did it to me." 41Then the Monarch will say to those on the left, "Depart from me, you cursed, into the eternal fire prepared for the devil and the devil's angels; 42for I was hungry and you gave me no food, I was thirsty and you gave me no drink, 43I was a stranger and you did not welcome me, naked and you did not clothe me, sick and in prison and you did not visit me." 44Then they also will answer, "O Sovereign,▢ when did we see you hungry or thirsty or a stranger or naked or sick or in prison, and did not minister to you?" 45Then the Monarch will answer them, "Truly, I say to you, as you did it not to one of the least of these, you did it not to me." 46And they will go away into eternal punishment, but the righteous into eternal life.

°RSV *Son of man.* See Appendix.
▢RSV *King.* See Appendix.
*Addition to the text. See "Metaphor" and "God the Father and Mother" in the Appendix.
*RSV *kingdom.* See Appendix.
▢RSV *Lord.* See Appendix.

Appendix

Metaphor

A metaphor is a figure of speech used to extend meaning through comparison of dissimilars. For example, "Life is a dream" is a metaphor. The character of dreams is ascribed to life, and the meaning of "life" is thus extended. "Dream" is used as a screen through which to view "life." Two dissimilars are juxtaposed.

The statement "God is Father" is also a metaphor. Two dissimilars, "Father" and "God," are juxtaposed, and so the meaning of "God" is extended. Although "God the Father" has been a powerful metaphor for communicating the nature of God, like any metaphor it can become worn. It may even be interpreted literally, that is, as describing exactly. The dissimilars become similar. The metaphor becomes a proposition.

Now, if one were to say "God is Mother," the power of the metaphor would be apparent. To offer the image "God the Mother and Father" as a lens through which to view God elicits the response of a true metaphor, just as the statement "God is Father" once did. In this lectionary, "God the Father and Mother" is used as a formal equivalent of "the Father" or "God the Father." "God the Father" is clearly a metaphor, just as "God the Mother" is. God is not a father, any more than God is a mother, or than life is a dream. By reading and hearing "God the Father and Mother" we provide a metaphor for God which balances the more familiar *male* imagery for God with *female* imagery. There are many female images for God in the scriptures, such as "As one whom his mother comforts, so I will comfort you" (Isa. 66:13), and the parable of the woman seeking the lost coin (Luke 15:8-10). Metaphors are figurative and open-ended. Their meanings vary from hearer to hearer, but they are not dispensable, for there is no other way by which to say directly what the metaphor communicates. A metaphor provides a new way of seeing.

(*) [*God*] the Father [*and Mother*] (RSV Father, God the Father, God our Father) or (⊗) God (RSV my Father, the Father)

One of the outstanding characteristics of the Christian faith is its emphasis on the personal nature of God. While God is also described in impersonal terms (Rock, Light, Love), personal imagery prevails.

"Father" is one such personal term: Jesus called God "Father." In fact, it has been argued that Jesus always addressed God as "Father" in his prayers, the single exception being Jesus' cry from the cross (Matt. 27:46; Mark 15:34, a quotation from Ps. 22). That Jesus frequently called God "Father" or "my Father" (cf. Mark 14:36) is an astonishing fact that obviously had great significance for him. God is rarely addressed as "Father" in the Old Testament. But for Jesus, *Abba* ("Father") was a sacred word, pointing to the mysterious intimacy Jesus had with God ("No one knows the Son except the Father, and no one knows the Father except the Son," Matt. 11:27), and pointing to the intimate relationship his disciples also had with God ("Call no one your father on earth, for you have one Father, who is in heaven," Matt. 23:9).

This terminology for God employed by Jesus is one evidence used by the earliest church to support its claim that Jesus was the *Christ*. Jesus "called God his own Father, making himself equal with God" (John 5:18; cf. 19:7). As Christians we have continued to hold that Jesus is uniquely the Child of God.

That Jesus called God "Father" is the basis for our thinking about Jesus Christ as one of the three Persons of the Trinity. As the words of the Nicene Creed state, Jesus Christ is "begotten, not made, being of one substance with the Father," a relationship which cannot be claimed by any created being. The relationship which the Father/Son imagery of the New Testament seeks to describe is that of Jesus being of the same substance as God. But if God the Son proceeded from God the Father alone, this procession is both a male and a female action, a begetting *and* a birth. God is the motherly father of the child who comes forth. It was the orthodox dogmatic tradition which most dramatically defended Trinitarian language about God, and it is this tradition which speaks most boldly of God's bisexuality. According to the Third Council of Toledo, "it must be held that the Son was created, neither out of nothingness nor yet out of any substance, but that He was begotten or born out of the Father's womb (*de utero Patris*), that is, out of His very essence."

The phrase used in this lectionary, "God the Father and Mother," is an attempt to express in a fresh way the same intimacy, caring, and freedom of Jesus' identification of God as *Abba*. It is also an attempt to hold on to the important Christian belief that Jesus is the Child of God. Just as we do not create our children, but give them birth out of our very selves, we believe that God did not create Jesus, but that God gave birth to Jesus.

It is also the case that Christians rejected as pagan the view that God is father of the world. For Christians, God is Father in relation to the Son. Christians are brought into this relationship because they are adopted as heirs (Rom. 8:15, 23; Gal. 4:5; Eph. 1:5).

God, the Almighty Father, considered as the author of all things, is a Zeus-like figure, sitting on Mt. Olympus, a remote and solitary power. Such an authoritarian God causes earthly authorities to take their cues from "Him." God as Almighty Father legitimates the authority of the fathers of the church, the father of the country, the father of the family.

This is not the way Jesus spoke of God as Father. *Abba* is an accessible, caring, revered figure.

The image of God as Father has been used to support the excessive authority of earthly fathers in a patriarchal social structure. The metaphor "God the Father and Mother" expresses the close relationship between language about God and language about the human community. The mutuality and coequality of the persons of the Trinity is a model for human community and especially appropriate, therefore, for readings prepared for worship. Those who worship in the Christian church are struggling to bring about a community where there is no longer male or female, but where all are one in Christ Jesus, and joint heirs according to the promise (Gal. 3:28). (See also Metaphor.) (NOTE: "God" substituted for "he" or "him" is not footnoted.)

(□) Sovereign, God the SOVEREIGN ONE, etc. (RSV Lord, LORD, etc.)

According to Hebrew tradition the personal name for God, *Yahweh*, was introduced by Moses at the time of the exodus. Sometime after 538 B.C. the name was no longer pronounced for fear that it would be profaned, even though it continued to be written in the text of the scriptures. From that time on, the chief word read in place of the divine name was *adonai*—an honorific title translated "my lord." In those places in the RSV where the underlying Hebrew text contains the divine name, and not simply the word *adonai*, the typography is changed to LORD. In this lectionary, the Hebrew word *elohim* is rendered "God," as in the RSV. Where the divine name (*Yahweh*) is found in the original (RSV "LORD"), it is rendered as "GOD" or "SOVEREIGN ONE." The latter equivalent is used especially where the name is emphasized or where literary concerns seem to make that wording preferable. Occasionally the divine name is found in combination with the word for God (*Yahweh elohim*) or with the word for Lord (*adonai Yahweh*). These are rendered in the RSV as "LORD God" and "Lord GOD," respectively. In this lectionary the former is rendered as "God the SOVEREIGN ONE," and the latter as "Sovereign GOD."

When the Old Testament was translated into Greek, *elohim* ("God") was translated by *theos*, meaning "God." Both the name *Yahweh* and the title *adonai* were translated by the word *kyrios*, meaning "Lord." It was the Greek translation of the Old Testament on which the New Testament authors basically relied. In the New Testament, therefore, the primary terms used to designate God are *theos* ("God") and *kyrios* ("Lord"); and the word *kyrios* was also taken over by the church as a primary way to designate Jesus: "Jesus is Lord."

Kyrios also has a wide range of other meanings. It is used for the *owner* of possessions, for the *head* of a family, or for the *master* of a house or of slaves. In the vocative it often means "Sir."

Kyrios has been translated into English by "Lord" (or "lord"), a word which in common usage means a man with power and authority, such as a titled nobleman. Its equivalent for a woman is "Lady" (or "lady").

Lord is clearly a biased translation when used to refer to God, who is beyond sexual identification. In reference to the earthly Jesus it is somewhat more appropriate, but it tends again toward bias when used for the risen Christ. The risen Christ is one with God, and language used to describe Christ should reflect this.

In this lectionary *kyrios* generally has been translated "Sovereign" ("sovereign"), a word that also means one supreme in power and authority. It intends no theological difference from "Lord," but is free of purely male identification. Women as well as men are sovereigns. Elizabeth II is currently sovereign of England.

"Sovereign" thus has another advantage for the translator over "Lord." It is a word in contemporary usage. Not only are there living sovereigns in monarchical societies but nations as well are said to exercise sovereignty.

Kyrios has a further important connotation. The designation of Jesus Christ as *kyrios* by the early Christians meant that for them Caesar was not *kyrios*. Christians have come to believe that Jesus Christ has authority even over all earthly authorities. Hence, the status of the authority of the *Sovereign Jesus Christ* in relation to any national sovereignty is expressed in a contemporary idiom which brings to the fore the revolutionary significance of the statement *Kyrios Iēsous* (Jesus is Lord [Sovereign]) for the history of the church.

(°) Child, Child of God (RSV Son, Son of God)

"Son" is used as a designation of Jesus as the Messiah (Matt. 1:1a; 9:27). At Jesus' baptism there was a voice from heaven: "This is my beloved Son" (Matt. 3:17). Jesus also refers to himself as "Son," though seldom except in the Gospel of John, where the self-designation is common.

A son is male issue (cf. Matt. 1:21); and of course the historical person, Jesus, was a man. But as the Gospels depict Jesus, his maleness is incidental to his humanity. That Jesus was a *male* person is not said to have any Christological significance for salvation, but that Jesus was *human* is crucial—both for Jesus' designation as the Christ and for Jesus' work of salvation.

If the fact that Jesus was a male has no Christological significance, then neither has the fact that Jesus was a *son* and not a *daughter*. Therefore, in this lectionary the formal equivalent "Child" or "Child of God" is used for "Son" when the latter has Christological significance. Occasionally various modifiers such as "your" or "that" are used with "Child" to avoid juvenile connotations. Also, the masculine pronouns "he" and "him," when referring to "Child" ("Son") are rendered "Child." Thus, female hearers of the lectionary readings will be enabled to identify themselves with Jesus' *humanity* just as male hearers do.

In traditional language, Jesus as "the Son" makes believers "sons" and therefore heirs. In this lectionary, Jesus as the Child of God makes believers—men and women—children of God and therefore heirs. When Jesus is called "Son of God" it is not Jesus' male character that is of primary importance but Jesus' intimate relationship with God (cf. Matt. 11:25-27). Other connotations of "sonship" are divine authority (cf. Matt. 28:18-20), eschatological revelation, and freedom (cf. Rom. 8:21). (NOTE: "Child" substituted for "he" or "him" is not footnoted.)

(°) Human One (RSV Son of man)

In this lectionary the formal equivalent of "the Son of man" is "the Human One." In Dan. 7:13, "one like a son of man" may also be translated "an apparently human figure"; so the Gospels' "the Son of man" may be rendered "the human figure" or "the Human One" as a title, laying aside the strictly male aspect of the phrase "the *Son* of *man*" and emphasizing the human connotations of the term.

(*) Realm of God (RSV Kingdom, Kingdom of God)

The Greek word usually translated "kingdom" in the Bible refers primarily to the exercise of royal authority and power, and secondarily to that area over which such rule is exercised. The word *realm* is used in this lectionary instead of the word *kingdom*; for example, "kingdom of God" is rendered *realm of God*. Likewise, the uniquely Matthean expression "the gospel of the kingdom" (Matt. 4:23; 9:35) has been rendered *the gospel of the realm of God*.

(□) Ruler; Monarch (RSV King)

The word "king" is used in the Bible both to refer to earthly royal figures and as a metaphor for God, emphasizing God's majesty and power.

In this lectionary "king" is usually translated as "monarch," and occasionally as "ruler." The word "monarch" is preferable to "ruler" as a translation for "king," since it indicates a single or primary ruler. Monarchs can be either male or female: Elizabeth II, Queen of England, is a monarch. In two parables "king" was retained because the stories are about a king, and "king" is not a metaphor for Jesus or God (Matt. 18:23-35; 22:1-14). (NOTE: The nouns "ruler" and "monarch" substituted for "he" or "him" are not footnoted.)

Sisters and Brothers, Friends, Neighbors (RSV Brother, Brethren)

The contemporary use of such phrases as "sisters and brothers in Christ" to address members of the church is helpful in clarifying how the words "brother" and "brethren" are used in the Bible. In Hebrew usage, the same word could refer to a sibling, a more distant relative, a neighbor, or a member of one's community or group. Paul appears to reflect such a broad use of the word "brethren" in Rom. 9:3, where "my brethren" (translated in this lectionary as "my own people") is parallel to "my kinsmen by race." In Greek "brother" was often used to refer to a friend, or one with whom one shares a common purpose beyond the immediate family.[1]

In the New Testament, the plural form of the word "brother" appears to have been intended to include both women and men. The plural form is commonly used to address the church at large, both in speaking (Luke 21:16) and in writing (examples in this lectionary, Rom. 8:12; 1 Cor. 2:1). In such cases of direct address, "brethren" has been rendered in this lectionary either as "sisters and brothers" or as "friends." In post-resurrection sayings attributed to Jesus, "brethren" is rendered as "followers" (Matt. 28:10) or "friends" (John 20:17), to make clear that the reference is to the nascent church and not to Jesus' siblings.

(*) Addition of Women's Names to the Text

In several instances, women's names have been added to the text in this lectionary. These names are offered where generation or origin of the people is the concern. The additional names therefore make explicit what was formerly implicit, namely, women's obvious role in childbearing. An example of this is Matt. 3:9, where the lectionary text reads "and do not presume to say to yourselves, 'We have Abraham as our father [*and Sarah and Hagar as our mothers*]'; for I tell you, God is able from these stones to

---

[1]See the discussion in W.F. Arndt and F.W. Gingrich, *A Greek-English Lexicon of the New Testament and Other Early Christian Literature*, Adelphos (4). For example, in Matthew, and especially in the Sermon on the Mount, the Greek word *adelphos* seems to carry the meaning of "neighbor" (Matt. 5:22, 23, 24; 18:15, 21).

raise up children to Abraham, [*Sarah, and Hagar*]." Although the people of Israel are not descendants of Hagar, nonetheless her descendants are also children of Abraham.

Other Exclusive Imagery: Slave, Darkness

Slave. The term "slave" designates one who is inferior to or in the service of another. In its literal sense it describes the inequality of a human relationship, and in some instances human bondage itself. In its religious usage it serves as a metaphor for the devotee's relationship to God and sometimes to wickedness and sin. In the Bible, service to God and one's neighbor is affirmed and placed upon a nonoppressive and nonexploitative plane. Because of this and because the continued use of the term "slave" recalls the rejected institution of chattel slavery and other oppressive class, racial, and sexual distinctions, this lectionary avoids using the term "slave" wherever possible.

Darkness. The biblical imagery of light versus darkness (John 1:5; Rom. 13:12) is often used to contrast good with evil. The equation of evil with darkness, or that which is done in secret and out of the light, has unfortunately led some persons and groups to condemn and reject anything that is black or any dark-hued person as evil or somehow condemned by God. This color symbolism has its equally inaccurate and unfortunate correlative in the equation of light with white—with what is true, good, and loved of God. For example, the William Bright hymn "And Now, O Father" has the line, "From tainting mischief keep them white and clear . . ." and in the Bible "wash me, and I shall be whiter than snow" (Ps. 51:7). While the biblical context may be free from racist intent, the too-easy misconception that dark people are also condemned and to be avoided has led to the use of terminology other than "darkness" as a metaphor for sin and evil in this lectionary.

Use of "They," "Them," and "Their" as Singular Pronouns

In a very few cases, the lectionary committee has made use of the pronouns "they," "them," or "their" with singular antecedents. There is much solid precedent for this usage: dramatists William Shakespeare and George Bernard Shaw, Lord Chesterfield, the late President John F. Kennedy, and Doris Lessing are among those careful speakers and writers who use that construction. *Webster's New Collegiate Dictionary* (G. & C. Merriam Co., 1973) states that "they" is "often used with an indefinite third person singular antecedent." *The Modern Language Association Handbook for Writers of Research Papers, Theses, and Dissertations* (1977) warns that careful writers "now avoid the use of the generic pronoun 'he' in referring to a person whose sex is not specified so as to avoid the possible implication that only a male person is intended." See Casey Miller and Kate Swift, *Words and Women: New Language in New Times* (1976).

Index of Readings for Year A

Based on the Lectionary of
The Consultation on Church Union

45:1-7	Pentecost 22
49:1-7	Epiphany 2
49:8-18	Epiphany 8
50:4-9a	Passion Sunday
52:6-10	Christmas Day (Third Proper)
52:13-53:12	Good Friday
55:1-5, 10-13	Pentecost 8
55:6-11	Pentecost 18
56:1-8	Pentecost 13
58:5-10	Epiphany 5
60:1-6	Epiphany
61:10-62:3	Christmas 2
62:6-12	Christmas Day (Second Proper)
63:7-9	Christmas 1

Jeremiah

15:15-21	Pentecost 15
20:7-13	Pentecost 5

Ezekiel

18:1-4, 25-32	Pentecost 19
33:1-11	Pentecost 16
34:11-17, 23-24	Last Sunday After Pentecost
37:1-14	Lent 5
39:21-29	Easter 7 (alternate)

Daniel

7:9-14	Ascension (alternate)

Hosea

5:15-6:6	Pentecost 3

Joel

2:12-19	Ash Wednesday
2:28-32	Pentecost

Amos

3:1-8	Epiphany 3 (alternate)
5:18-24	Pentecost 26

Micah

6:1-8	Epiphany 4

Zephaniah

1:7, 12-18	Pentecost 27
2:3; 3:11-13	Epiphany 4 (alternate)

Zechariah

9:9-13	Pentecost 7

Malachi

1:4b-2:10	Pentecost 24

Wisdom of Solomon [Apocrypha]

6:12-16	Pentecost 26 (alternate)
12:13; 13:16-19	Pentecost 9 (alternate)

Ecclesiasticus (Sirach) [Apocrypha]

15:15-20	Epiphany 6 (alternate)
24:1-2, 8-12	Christmas 2 (alternate)
27:30-28:7	Pentecost 17 (alternate)

Matthew

1:18-25	Advent 4
2:1-12	Epiphany
2:13-15, 19-23	Christmas 2
3:1-12	Advent 2
3:13-17	Baptism of Our Sovereign
4:1-11	Lent 1
4:12-23	Epiphany 3
5:1-12	Epiphany 4
5:13-20	Epiphany 5
5:21-37	Epiphany 6
5:38-48	Epiphany 7
6:1-6, 16-21	Ash Wednesday
6:24-34	Epiphany 8
7:15-29	Pentecost 2
9:9-13	Pentecost 3
9:35-10:15	Pentecost 4
10:16-33	Pentecost 5
10:34-42	Pentecost 6
11:2-11	Advent 3
11:25-30	Pentecost 7
13:1-23	Pentecost 8
13:24-43	Pentecost 9
13:44-52	Pentecost 10
14:13-21	Pentecost 11
14:22-33	Pentecost 12
15:21-28	Pentecost 13
16:13-20	Pentecost 14

16:21-28	Pentecost 15
17:1-9	Epiphany 9
18:15-20	Pentecost 16
18:21-35	Pentecost 17
20:1-16	Pentecost 18
21:28-32	Pentecost 19
21:33-43	Pentecost 20
22:1-14	Pentecost 21
22:15-22	Pentecost 22
22:34-46	Pentecost 23
23:1-12	Pentecost 24
24:36-44	Advent 1
25:1-13	Pentecost 26
25:14-30	Pentecost 27
25:31-46	Last Sunday After Pentecost
26:14-27:66	Passion Sunday
28:1-10	Easter (alternate)
28:16-20	Ascension; Trinity

Luke

2:1-20	Christmas Day (First and Second Propers)
24:13-35	Easter 3
24:44-53	Ascension (alternate)

John

1:1-18	Christmas Day (Third Proper); Christmas 1
1:29-41	Epiphany 2
3:1-17	Lent 2
4:5-42	Lent 3
9:1-41	Lent 4
10:1-10	Easter 4
11:1-53	Lent 5
13:1-17, 34	Maundy Thursday
14:1-14	Easter 5
14:15-21	Easter 6
17:1-11	Easter 7
18:1-19:42	Good Friday
20:1-18	Easter
20:19-23	Pentecost
20:19-31	Easter 2

Acts

1:1-11	Ascension
1:1-14	Easter 7
2:1-21	Pentecost
2:14a, 22-32	Easter 2
2:14a, 36-47	Easter 3
6:1-9, 7:2a, 51-56	Easter 4
8:4-8, 14-17	Easter 6 (alternate)
10:34-38	Baptism of Our Sovereign
10:34-48	Easter
17:1-15	Easter 5
17:22-31	Easter 6

Romans

1:1-7	Advent 4
3:21-28	Pentecost 2
4:1-9; 13-17	Lent 2
4:13-25	Pentecost 3
5:1-11	Lent 3
5:6-11	Pentecost 4
5:12-21	Lent 1; Pentecost 5
6:1-11	Pentecost 6
7:15-8:13	Pentecost 7
8:6-19	Lent 5
8:18-25	Pentecost 8
8:26-27	Pentecost 9
8:28-30	Pentecost 10
8:31-39	Pentecost 11
9:1-5	Pentecost 12
11:13-16, 29-32	Pentecost 13
11:33-36	Pentecost 14
12:1-8	Pentecost 15
12:9-13:10	Pentecost 16
13:8-14	Advent 1
14:5-12	Pentecost 17
15:4-13	Advent 2

1 Corinthians

1:1-9	Epiphany 2
1:10-17	Epiphany 3
1:18-31	Epiphany 4
2:1-5	Epiphany 5
2:6-13	Epiphany 6
3:10-11, 16-23	Epiphany 7
4:1-13	Epiphany 8
11:17-32	Maundy Thursday
15:20-28	Last Sunday After Pentecost

2 Corinthians

5:20b-6:10	Ash Wednesday
13:5-14	Trinity

Galatians		*Titus*	
4:4-7	Christmas 1	2:11-15	Christmas Day (First Proper)
		3:4-7	Christmas Day (Second Proper)
Ephesians			
1:3-6, 15-23	Christmas 2		
1:15-23	Ascension	*Hebrews*	
3:1-12	Epiphany	1:1-12	Christmas Day (Third Proper)
5:8-14	Lent 4	4:14-16; 5:7-9	Good Friday
		10:1-25	Good Friday (alternate)
Philippians			
1:1-11, 19-27	Pentecost 18		
2:1-13	Pentecost 19	*James*	
2:5-11	Passion Sunday	5:7-10	Advent 3
3:12-21	Pentecost 20		
4:4-20	Pentecost 21	*1 Peter*	
		1:3-9	Easter 2
Colossians		1:17-23	Easter 3
3:1-11	Easter	2:1-10	Easter 5
		2:19-25	Easter 4
1 Thessalonians		3:8-22	Easter 6
1:1-5a	Pentecost 22	4:12-19	Easter 7
1:5b-2:8	Pentecost 23		
2:7-13, 17-20	Pentecost 24	*2 Peter*	
4:13-18	Pentecost 26	1:16-21	Epiphany 9
5:1-11	Pentecost 27		